Sociological Theory

An Introduction to the
Classical Tradition

Sociological Theory

*An Introduction to the
Classical Tradition*

RICHARD W. HADDEN

broadview press

CANADIAN CATALOGUING IN PUBLICATION DATA

Hadden, Richard W. (Richard William)
    Sociological theory: an introduction to the classical tradition

Includes bibliographical references and index.
ISBN 1-55111 095-4

1. Sociology – Philosophy.   2. Sociology – History
1. Title

BM24.H3226 1997   301'.01   C97-930453-9

broadview press
Post Office Box 1243, Peterborough, Ontario, Canada K9J 7H5

in the United States of America:
3576 California Road, Orchard Park, NY 14127

in the United Kingdom:
Turpin Distribution Services Ltd., Blackhorse Rd.,
Letchworth, Hertfordshire SG6 1HN

broadview press gratefully acknowledges the support of the Canada Council, the Ontario Arts Council, and the Ministry of Canadian Heritage.

PRINTED IN CANADA

10 9 8 7 6 5 4 3

CONTENTS

ACKNOWLEDGEMENTS

THE AUTHOR would like to thank first of all his Saint Mary's Sociology 362 students who have lived through his trials of various materials. Their impressions and responses are embodied in countless ways in this effort. To those from whom I have learned much about theory, Berkeley Fleming, Roy Hornosty and Cyril Levitt, I owe an immeasurable debt. Three anonymous reviewers for Broadview Press also provided helpful comments. Several friends and colleagues have also responded to my requests for comments and provided a sounding board when I needed to think out loud: Jane Bagnall, Mike McConkey, Ginger McNevin, Kiran Mirchandani, Michael Overington, Mike Vance and Henry Veltmeyer. Michael Harrison of Broadview Press has been helpful and patient above and beyond the call of duty. Many thanks to Angela Dinaut for compiling the index.

PREFACE

THIS WORK is intended to serve the purpose of introducing undergraduate sociology students to the main themes and arguments of the "founding fathers" (dead white guys) of sociological thought. Either as extensions of or as counters to these themes and arguments, contemporary thought and the teaching of it must, in my view, rest on a clear (rather than playful or narrowly focused) presentation of the classical thinkers' fundamental concepts.

This is, furthermore, a rather brief treatment of some major and complex issues. Its brevity is necessary in order to fulfil its function as a companion either to readings of the original works of Marx, Durkheim, and Weber or to other more focused interpretations. Although I deem it worthwhile, challenging, and rewarding to introduce students at a second or third year level to selections from original works (i.e. to writings not designed for them), these cannot stand alone as sufficient and appropriate materials for an introductory undergraduate course in classical sociological theory.

The standard approach to the teaching of classical theory in the North American curriculum involves the use of a single, secondary, all-inclusive, expensive text. This has its advantages: an even, unified treatment; a student-centred style; and a ready-made plan for the course of study over a single semester. For many, however, the "thick" secondary text also has its drawbacks: satisfying no one's curiosity in its attempt to please everyone's; costing too much; and presenting a superficially unified melange of too many themes and authors.

In the past nine years of teaching a one-semester course in classical theory by using primary readings, I have been frustrated by the difficulty of relying solely on primary texts (a daunting task for most students) in the face of the lack of a suitable, inexpensive, brief, secondary text to introduce these readings and to provide students with the comfort of an easily readable version of the chief concepts and arguments involved.

In this vein, the text is intended to serve two main purposes: clarity and flexibility. To the extent that it succeeds in providing a clear, "boiled down" version of those fundamental concepts and arguments, without doing too much violence to their richness, it will also provide instructors with the flexibility required for them to "take off" in whatever direction they may wish with respect to interpretations, emphases, and additional materials and arguments.

It is my hope to present a clear version of fundamental concepts and arguments which will enable a rich variety of subsequent themes and foci, materials, and frameworks to be explored. Instructors with varying interpretations should, I hope, be able to employ this work to help establish a foundation, and then to pursue their own lines of inquiry, complete with appropriate materials, primary or secondary. A clear presentation of fundamentals in a brief secondary text enables the flexible selection of issues and materials.

INTRODUCTION

When we hear the word "theory" it does not usually invoke a lot of enthusiasm. First of all, the term suggests a rather dry, heavy and complex set of statements and claims which comprise a less than certain knowledge. On the one hand, we have theory and, on the other, facts, certainty, reality. Why not simply deal with the latter? A course in sociological theory is not often awaited with great expectation. Yet, when we feel that we have a reasonable, cogent, and even well-worked-out bit of knowledge about a particular part of the world, it inevitably entails an entire set of assumptions about how the world basically operates and about what knowledge is. In other words, consciously or not, we employ a framework. A course in sociological theory is an occasion to purposefully explore the frameworks themselves. In classical sociological theory, we look at the frameworks, accounts, concepts, and arguments of those who initially founded the discipline.

Since we inevitably employ sets of assumptions and hypothetical inferences, it will serve us well to examine them explicitly. It would be premature to develop our own framework, but it is appropriate to become familiar with the frameworks of those who have gone before us, have produced accounts of our world which are thorough, and have had some lasting influence on subsequent thought. The work of the founders of the discipline is still consulted, even though no one believes their ideas to be correct on all accounts. This exercise is one of the best ways to check and "try out" our own notions of the social world.

This text presents a brief version of the major concepts and arguments of some of the founders of sociology. It is designed to be used with a collection of original selections or with other, more focused, secondary texts. It starts with a brief examination of the ideas of the Enlightenment, Conservative Reaction, Comte, and Spencer. The choice of starting point is somewhat arbitrary. One could start with the political thought of the Greeks or with the contract theorists of the early modern period. The Enlightenment is chosen because this type of thought is an indicator that modern society, not just a novel set of ideas, has arrived. This period also heralds the arrival of a new discipline, sociology. The fundamental approach and the concepts of sociology are begun in the period of the Enlightenment and Conservative Reaction. Questions about the relation between the individual and society and about the means of investigating it are raised in a lasting way.

Comte and Spencer were, for the most part, the first sociologists. Their concerns were with the means and path of societal development, and the conditions for harmony and continued development. They present quite different views on these issues, and a comparison of their work sets the stage for the discussion of the "big three" founders, Karl Marx, Emile Durkheim, and Max Weber.

In Marx's view, the most important thing about a people is their practical life-activity. The way a people produce for themselves gives shape to other aspects of their society and culture. The way they relate to nature and the way they are related to one another in society are the most fundamental sets of relations. These sets of relations change and develop over the course of history. They change from one "mode of production" to another. We now live in what is termed the "capitalist mode of production," and most of Marx's work is devoted to investigating the primary features of this set of relations. In his view, they are not harmonious or reasonably ordered, and he searches for indications that they might change into a new set which is more reasonable.

Durkheim is more inclined to find harmony, and he attempts to uncover the essential features of collective life which are responsible for producing it. He determines that there is a realm of "social facts," ways of thinking, acting, and feeling which are produced by group existence and which tend to produce an integrated society. Modern society is the product of the development of the division of labour, and its recent complexity presents some problems for integration; however, Durkheim is confident that he has found the essential features of harmonious, collective life which will allow sociology to intervene on its behalf.

Weber views the development of modern society as a much less orderly affair and is rather pessimistic about the possibility of discovering some means of harmonizing its present condition. He attempts to understand various institutions and states of society in terms of the actions of individuals. His central concept for this purpose is "social action." He analyzes organizations of individuals in different positions on the basis of their motivations. These, in turn, rest on subjective meanings which persons attach to the things and other persons in their environment. On this basis, he examines the relation between forms of authority, social organization, and the economic distribution of rewards. He is pessimistic about the bureaucratic form of domination found in modern society; in his view, it is a very stable form of the domination of powerful interests. We conclude with a brief comparison of Marx, Durkheim, and Weber's views of modern society.

I

The Enlightenment,
Conservative Reaction,
Comte and Spencer

THE ENLIGHTENMENT

THE ENLIGHTENMENT, the collective name for the thought of a group of radical thinkers in mid-eighteenth century France, is most readily characterizable as "liberal individualism." The Enlightenment emphasized the individual's possession of critical reason, and it was opposed to traditional authority in society and the primacy of religion in questions of knowledge.

The use of "enlightenment" as a name for a perspective or world-view may appear to us to be an attempt to prejudice our attention in its favour. Who, after all, would prefer to be left in the dark? But written with a capital "E", this term refers to a specific movement of thought in eighteenth century France. Its participants battled against the prejudice, superstition, ignorance, and tyranny they saw manifested in their world.

These thinkers, most of whom are referred to collectively as the Philosophes, vehemently opposed authority in government and religion, but most of all in knowledge. They were not the first in Europe to produce, promote, and recommend changes in the sorts of knowledge deemed valid. Renaissance humanism, the "scientific revolution" of the sixteenth and seventeenth centuries, and the establishment of scientific (natural philosophical) societies in England, France, Holland, and Italy had already set the stage for the ascendency of "reason," the buzz-word of the Enlightenment.

Francis Bacon (1561-1626) had attacked the older philosophy of the scholastics (a philosophy derived primarily from

Aristotle [384-22 B.C.E.] and amended by Aquinas [c.1225-74] and others); Hobbes (1588-1679) had declared that reason was found in equal measure in all men. Bacon feared a civil war; it eventually came about (1641-43) in England after his death. During this war, Hobbes found safety in Holland and France. Giordano Bruno (1548-1600) had been burned at the stake for his heretical views; Galileo (1564-1642) lived out the last years of his life under a virtual "house arrest"; and Descartes (1596-1650), fearing a similar fate, also spent a good deal of his life in Holland.

Although no one wanted to be left in the dark, to remain ignorant, what was at issue was precisely the definitions of light and of darkness. What was light for some, appeared as darkness and as dangerous to others. Furthermore, when people are killed for their beliefs, flee their homelands for safety, or have their ideas and writings monitored, others, we may assume, feel threatened. Bacon and Bruno are figures of the sixteenth century; Hobbes, Descartes, and Galileo of the seventeenth. The Philosophes of the eighteenth century were able to flex a bit of muscle in the name of reason. Reason was set in opposition to two other terms: on the one hand to "authority," any person or body deemed to hold traditionally legitimate sway over the beliefs and actions of others; and, on the other, to "revelation," the specific form, according to the Church, in which knowledge was said to be delivered to humankind. (God, according to this view, is said to reveal knowledge to humans through the Church.)

Reason and revelation had already been engaged in battle before the Enlightenment. In the context of eighteenth century France, however, the battle emerged as a major political challenge to authority. In other words, to undermine the authority of Church and State over the everyday lives of ordinary folk, Enlightenment thinkers proposed, not to take up arms and storm the centres of sacred and secular power, but to attack and criticize conceptions of knowledge. Of utmost importance in this political/intellectual project was the conviction that everyone came into the world in possession of a full-blown faculty of reason. If allowed full use and exercise of this faculty (i.e. if no tyrannical force interfered with their

thinking and decision-making processes), they could successfully employ this reason to decide adequately on all courses
of action required for daily life: political, social, moral, economic or material.

This insistence on the ability of people to act rationally,
of course, was anathema to Church and State. A consensus
about ideas, beliefs, and knowledge provides comfort, in the
sense of a reliable view of the world and of our action within
it. If virtually everyone, at least in a given nation or society,
were to view the world and the nature of everything in it in
a particular, coherent fashion (the view, say of the Church),
then everyone could rely on the expectation that others, too,
would see the world in a recognizable and familiar way. We
could all go about our business as usual, confident that the
behaviour of others would provide us with few surprises. If,
however, a particular world-view or set of ideas appears to
be forced upon us, and if this kind of world and our position
and action within it are not to our liking but benefit those
whose ideas are being forced upon us, then conflict about
ideas *and* conditions may well ensue.

What came to be at issue in eighteenth century France,
therefore, was the question of exactly whose view of the
world, and of action within it, was to be accepted. If knowledge were seen as delivered by God to officials of the Church
and if this knowledge referred to a hierarchy of "estates,"
each with a different nature and a different set of capabilities
and faculties, then we can begin to see why someone who
felt that everyone possessed the same faculties, and that many
were oppressed in the current state of affairs, would object
to the notion of knowledge as revelation.

According to the received view, there existed a Great Chain
of Being (see Lovejoy 1960). Everything in the world was
arranged in a hierarchy from highest (God) to lowest (rocks).
In the middle of this hierarchy, society itself was divided into
estates from highest (nobility and clergy) to lowest (serfs and
peasants), and each was seen as naturally superior or inferior
to the other.

As society itself changed from this feudal, medieval condition, and as the notion of fundamental, human equality

became more popular, it also seemed less absurd or bizarre to challenge both earthly authority and the notion of knowledge (revelation) which supported this view of society. From the fourteenth through the seventeenth centuries, in various parts of Europe, feudalism (the arrangement of estates in the countryside) fell, cities grew, commerce developed rapidly, and nation states came to supplant the former proliferation of local principalities. As it became more difficult for the Church to suggest that the hierarchical arrangement of estates was natural, so too did temporal, secular authority have a harder time justifying its traditional sway over people (divine right of kings). With the actual fall of feudalism, it became very difficult to argue that its preferential arrangement of classes or estates was natural.

In the seventeenth and eighteenth centuries, however, it was still seen as radical to claim that those at the bottom of the proverbial ladder were in possession of reason in equal measure to those at the top. Knowledge, adequate to the making of everyday decisions with regard to both nature and society, was seen by the Philosophes to be obtainable by all. How to build a bridge, plant and nurture a crop, relate properly to one's fellow humans, or any other practical question which might arise was seen by Enlightenment thinkers as answerable by means of the free employment of one's reason, rather than by reliance on the word and power of any established authority. According to this view, knowledge is not delivered to people but obtained by them. For Mary Wollstonecraft, author of *A Vindication of The Rights of Woman* (1974)[1797], this was a maxim. In her hands, the notion of universal equality was even more consistently applied. She especially recommended the education of women. All necessary knowledge is learnable by all.

This was not simply an arcane, closely argued and specialized philosophical insight. These thinkers were not professional academics desiring to publish in order to advance their careers. Such new and radical notions were part of a political agenda designed to play a role in the overthrow of traditional authority. This was intellectual warfare: the undermining of authority by challenging its fundamental ideas, particularly its idea of knowledge.

Every individual, it was thought, could discover for him/herself if a notion were true or false, adequate or useless. If only we were allowed the use of our own innate, critical reason, we could find out for ourselves. "Think For Yourself!" became the slogan of the Enlightenment. How was this to be accomplished since people were accustomed to relying on the authoritative word of State and Church, to being told how and what to think?

As well as the writing of several dictionaries, the crowning achievement of the Philosophes, directed by Denis Diderot and Jean Le Rond d'Alembert, was the compiling of the *Encyclopédie*, a compendious collection of extant theoretical and practical knowledge. (The following discussion of Enlightenment thought is heavily indebted to Lucien Goldmann's excellent *Philosophy of The Enlightenment*)

The new forms of knowledge were to be made as accessible as possible. Those who could read, or have someone read to them, were invited to avail themselves of a new source of knowledge which they could, in principle at least, check for themselves. This knowledge was to be as comprehensive as possible and to be presented in alphabetical order. They knew that knowledge had its own internal connections, but for purposes of accessible presentation, alphabetical order would suffice.

Thus for the Philosophes, knowledge, like reason itself, was a property of the individual. Individuals came into the world with their faculty of reason and acted *as* individuals by means of the knowledge gained from the use of this reason, hence, the characterization of the philosophy of the Enlightenment as "individualism." Knowledge was seen as an independent production of individual reason and practice or action was seen to follow *after* the acquisition of such knowledge. Knowledge was to be free from the influence of authority or prejudice and subsequently *applied* to nature or society. Human reason was seen as having limits but not as in need of any correction by faith. Individual consciousness was seen as the absolute origin of knowledge and action. The Philosophes advocated the free employment of critical reason, the acquisition of knowledge untainted by authority or prejudice, and the application of this knowledge to nature or society. There is no authority higher than individual reason. The basic, necessary ingredients for this progress of knowledge and action are already contained within the individual; the political and intellectual projects of the Philosophes were thought to be necessary simply to allow reason to begin functioning more fully. For the Philosophes, the possession of critical reason had always been *the* fundamental characteristic of the human individual; the Philosophes attempted to demonstrate this truth and to ensure its free reign in public life.

The Enlightenment's program of liberal individualism is thus based on the notion of a freely reasoning, independent, autonomous human individual. They would argue that these traits are fundamental to the nature of the human being; humans simply have not often been allowed, due to the presence of tyrannical authority, to function freely in this manner. How, we might ask, did these thinkers arrive at such a notion since tyranny and prejudice reigned supreme in their milieu? Did they perhaps see something in their world which provided them with an illustration of the fundamental autonomy of the human individual?

Enlightenment thinkers might answer that they used their own critical reason to derive this lasting truth. Goldmann (1973: 15-18) suggests that there was a rapidly growing sphere of contemporary society (the market) in which individuals actually interacted in such a way as to indicate some degree of autonomy. For Goldmann (1973: 18), the autonomous individual, relatively unconstrained by collectivity, tradition, community, the sacred, or authority is the exception rather than the rule; s/he is a product of history rather than its "point of departure." During what is by far the largest part of our history, individuals have not partaken of such autonomy. We have, by and large, been bound in communities by necessity, custom, and belief. In most past societies, the notion of an individual free to choose his/her own course of action would probably be seen as bizarre, if not absurd. There is, however, a sphere of human interaction and activity which fairly recently has grown to constitute a primary sphere of modern activity. The exchange of goods, market activity, has recently grown to become the dominant form in which we satisfy wants and needs. It is in this sphere that we appear, at least to some extent, to act as autonomous, independent individuals. For Goldmann, it is a view of the individual in the context of this kind of activity which predisposed the Philosophes to consider the human individual as naturally autonomous and as characterized by the possession of critical reason.

It is in this realm of activity that we actually find people engaged in negotiations, "making deals." Relations between persons in this area take on the form of *contracts* and are no longer governed so much by considerations of status. Striking agreements with others about prices, wages, work hours, for example, is the kind of activity in which we, in fact, exhibit something like autonomous decision-making. At least in this sphere, many of our relations and interactions have the character of negotiations. Negotiations, if they are to be truly negotiations, demand the existence of a relatively autonomous, thinking, free and equal individual. In Goldmann's view, the free, autonomous, independent individual emerges as the product of history, the history, in particular, of the development of exchange, of a market society. *Contract*, a free agreement between autonomous individuals, thus emerges as one of the fundamental concepts of Enlightenment thought. Many thinkers (Hobbes, Locke and Rousseau, for example) chose to see society and/or the state as themselves the result of a contract, an agreement between individuals.

An essential condition of such a free agreement is the fundamental *Equality* between the parties to the agreement. Neither sellers nor buyers, for example, could be seen as having some basic advantage over one another by virtue of a higher status. Therefore, the personal character of either party was to be considered irrelevant to such interactions. *Universality* thus emerges as another important concept of Enlightenment thought. *Toleration* was also a very important concept. One's religious convictions, for example, were irrelevant. Put rather differently, religious fanaticism was bad for business. Anyone was free to engage in contracts. *Freedom* was also seen as an indispensable feature of this kind of social relation.

Lastly, if we are to dispose of goods in relations of exchange, we must necessarily have something to dispose of; we must have some *Property*. We must have *private* property in the important sense that we are free to dispose of it as we wish. This notion is not as obvious as it may at first appear and has not always been the case. Property, as with land, for example, under Roman Law was sometimes restricted in terms of its disposal.

The term "liberal individualism," has been used as a brief description of Enlightenment thought. The individual is seen as the location and source of all the important ingredients in a "liberated" society. Social evils could be eliminated by recourse to critical reason located in the individual; through the acquisition of knowledge and its application to material production and to public and social affairs, the good society was to be secured. Attacks on tyranny, prejudice, authority, and religion were the order of the day for Enlightenment thinkers.

Critical reason, located in an autonomous individual, was central to the Enlightenment thinkers who proceeded to establish the significance of the following concepts: the contract, equality, universality, toleration, freedom, and property. These were seen as intellectual weapons in a struggle against secular and ecclesiastical authority and tyranny. It drew from and helped support an emerging commercial and industrial society.

As one might expect, the authority figures of the day did not take all of this "sitting down." They, too, had supporters who wrote treatises in their defense. Since these figures were, after all, in authority, they were well-placed to support a spirited defense of their position and the view of the world which supported it. In France, the main figures engaged in this defense were Bonald and Maistre; in England, this task fell to Edmund Burke.

THE CONSERVATIVE REACTION

BONALD, MAISTRE, and Burke were part of a movement against the Enlightenment labelled the conservative reaction. While Enlightenment thinkers are generally considered to be the intellectual forebears of the French Revolution (1789-94), the thinkers participating in the conservative reaction opposed this thought and, after the Revolution, sought to reverse or minimize its effects. In other words, what began as an intellectual, ideological assault on authority did conclude in an armed and bloody struggle; the Bastille was in fact stormed. Debate continues to this day about the proper interpretation of the legacy of the French Revolution. The thought of Bonald and Maistre attests to the ongoing opposition to the Enlightenment in France; across the channel in England, Edmund Burke responded in no uncertain terms with his *Reflections on The Revolution in France* (1955)[1797].

These thinkers maintained, with varying emphasis, the significance of tradition, authority, community, and the sacred in human, collective life. From this perspective, Burke responded with horror to the results of the French Revolution. For him, there must be and always had been an authority higher than the individual. The notion that individual reason could "reinvent" life on a continuing basis was viewed by him as absolutely absurd, and the belief in this notion could only result in dangerous confusion. Collective entities were important in the maintenance of any existence which could be called human. Tradition, authority, and community were thus viewed as indispensable to human life. Burke saw community as the resting place of the human soul. Some of the conservatives saw the role of the sacred as fundamental in all of this; other, more secular, thinkers did not.

What is most significant for our purposes is that the two sides in this debate each contributed substantially to the foundation of sociological thought. On the one side, we have Enlightenment liberal individualism with its emphasis on reason, individual freedom, contractual relations, and a reverence for science as the way to examine all spheres of experience, including the social. On the other, we have a conservative collectivism which emphasizes extra-individual concepts and entities. Social order, for these thinkers, is not reducible to the characteristics of its parts, individuals. The individual, reason, freedom, contract, science, and progressive change may be seen as those concepts representing the contribution of Enlightenment thought. The community, authority, tradition, and the sacred can be seen as the contribution from the conservative, collectivist side.

From the liberal Enlightenment view, there emerges a picture of a rational, scientific approach to all subject matter, natural or social. By locating all important characteristics, especially reason and action, in the individual, however, the Enlightenment appears to provide little appropriate subject matter for the discipline of sociology. Few of its major concepts and few of the entities identified in its arguments are social or collective in character. Thus while sociology acquires much of its rationalist approach to society from liberal thought, it had to rely on the conservative tradition for its subject matter, including society, community, tradition, and authority, in short, collective matters.

Sociology, it has been argued (e.g., Nisbet 1966: 21-44), thus represents a combination of liberal and conservative traditions of thought. It was liberal in its basic approach and in its respect for progressive change, but conservative in its emphasis on order and stability. In fact, this intellectual approach has been interpreted as the outcome of two different revolutions occurring in France and England around the turn of the nineteenth century, the French and Industrial revolutions. In France, the armed struggle against tyrannical authority resulted in such controversial events as "the Terror." Tremendous dislocations resulted from the attempt to democratize French society. In England, after the revolutions in the early 1640s and again in 1688, a less bloody but no less dislocating transformation took place in the form of the Industrial Revolution (from roughly 1780-1850). In each country, an aristocracy was displaced, or at least transformed, and fundamental relations between persons were forever changed. Even those who favoured a progressive, industrial society were ill at ease over the chaos and dislocations caused by revolutionary change.

Thus actual change in society helped to inspire and encourage a change in the forms of analysis and thought about society and social institutions. Many were vehemently in favour of an industrial society, but even these were anxious to help establish a more stable social order. A properly sociological form of thought began to emerge from this mixture. Rationalist, scientific, and systematically empirical forms of analysis were employed to examine the nature of institutions, communities, and politics, in short, society. Sociology might be seen as employing a liberal approach to a conservative subject matter. The terms, "liberal" and "conservative," however, must be used with caution. Historians are accustomed to criticizing sociologists, with some justification, for indiscriminately using such terms without reference to historical context. A term which has conservative connotations in one historical context may well be liberal in another (e.g. Marx's emphasis on collective notions as opposed to Burke's). In general, however, an approach stemming from an interest in individual freedom and reason, as well as the promotion of a new industrial society was applied to a concern with social order and stability. Order and stability came to be the aims of a form of analysis having its origins in more individualist concepts and arguments.

AUGUSTE COMTE (1798-1857)

Auguste Comte was born in France during the height of that period referred to above as chaotic and unstable. To add to the instability in his own immediate milieu, his parents were devout Catholics and ardent royalists. These were not affiliations conducive to one's personal safety.

The young Comte was an extraordinary student, excelling primarily in math and physics, and was able to demonstrate unusual feats of memory such as reading a page of text and immediately reciting it backwards by heart. His early career was a poorly organized and rather self-destructive affair in which he proceeded to "shoot himself in the foot" several times. Along with fourteen others, he was expelled from school after a student uprising over a geometry instructor, thus dashing hopes of an otherwise promising academic career.

He did, nonetheless, manage to become secretary to Henri St. Simon, another prominent thinker with whom Comte shared many ideas. He met, and later married, a nineteen-year-old prostitute; had a falling out with St. Simon; organized a subscription series of lectures on "The Positive Philosophy"; suffered from an eventually unhappy marriage; attempted suicide by throwing himself into the Seine River and was rescued by a passer-by, interpreting this good Samaritan act as a sign that his mission in life was to complete and disseminate his positive philosophy.

In 1829, Comte completed the series of lectures, and between 1830 and 1842, published his *Cours de Philosophie Positive* in six volumes. In 1832, he managed to achieve a minor appointment at the Ecole Polytechnique, but, in 1844, he wrote a scathing attack on St. Simon and the Ecole and was dismissed. During the same year, two other important events also occurred. Comte obtained a small stipend from the English philosopher, John Stuart Mill, who had been impressed by his *Positive Philosophy*, and he also began an affair with Madame Clotilde de Vaux. In 1846, she died in his arms and Comte was later to credit her with teaching him about the affective tendencies of human nature, a consideration which was to inform his suggestion for a "religion of humanity."

In fact, Comte was to see this religion of humanity as part of the practical application of his philosophy as recommended in his *The System of Positive Polity or Treatise of Sociology Instituting The Religion of Humanity*. *The Positive Philosophy* was the work in which he outlined his preferred way of knowing the world, and *The Positive Polity* contained his ideas about how to improve society, how to establish what was, in his view, the best society possible by applying this knowledge.

According to Comte, a stable social order rested on a consistent form of thought. He saw his own thought as leading to the establishment of a more stable, industrial order. He saw this relationship between thought and practice as a natural affinity rather than a causal one and saw thought as evolving naturally toward the kind of philosophy which he was formulating and recommending. Ways of thinking, of philosophizing, of knowing the world, were, in his view, primary, both in the history of humankind and in his own practice. In other words, Comte believed that people acted in such a way as to correspond with the way they thought. In different societies or periods of history, furthermore, a people's way of thinking, of knowing their world, was responsible, according to Comte, for producing the kind of society in which they lived.

THE LAW OF THREE STAGES

COMTE'S FIRST major publication was *A Prospectus of the Scientific Operations Required for the Reorganization of Society*, which he referred to as the "great discovery of the year, 1822."

In this work, we get a good glimpse of his entire program. It is here that he announces the plan for an empirical science of society and introduces his "law of three stages," the notion that the history of societies can be divided rather neatly into three distinct periods and that each kind of society is produced and supported by a different form of thought or way of doing philosophy. Since the society of his day was experiencing a period of crisis, of disorganization, he set out to discover the causes or reasons for this phenomenon, and he based his explanation on the difficult transition from one form of thought to another.

For Comte, evolution or progress was a matter concerning the growth of the human mind. The human mind evolved through a series of stages, each of which marked a significantly different way of thinking or philosophizing. The mind, not the brain but our way of thinking or knowing, developed from a theological stage, through a metaphysical stage, and, finally, to a positive stage. He viewed the period in which he lived in France as the difficult transition to the final or positive stage. This transition was difficult, he thought, because near the end of one stage of the mind's growth, the form of society which is based on and supported by a particular form of thought, will undergo a period of disorganization as the society prepares to reorganize anew, based on the newly emerging form of thought.

In Comte's view, there is an affinity or correspondence between a way of thinking and a particular form of society. The first stage of the mind, which he called theological or fictitious, was marked by an understanding of the world in terms of supernatural beings, and those experiencing this stage did not approach phenomena with the aid of any hypotheses or preparatory theory. Events were explained during this stage by means of the action of many gods.

Theological thought provided the intellectual and moral basis, Comte argued, for a militaristic society. Here he evokes images of warlike, tribal societies with a polytheistic worldview. Of primary importance in Comte's scheme, remember, is the notion of the affinity between way of thinking, on the one hand, and form of society, on the other. Ways of thinking are primary and tend to support or provide the basis for a particular kind of society. In other words, a given way of doing philosophy will support or fit with one form of society better than some other.

Comte referred to the next stage as metaphysical. In this stage, the many gods or supernatural beings were replaced by one God and abstract entities. Medieval European philosophy, for example, was full of abstract concepts, such as real entities, that were seen to lie behind phenomena. This was a rational attempt to account for all worldly phenomena by means of metaphysics, that which is beyond the physical. According to this view, there was a rational, reasonable world, but it was not observable in the phenomena themselves. One had to speculate about rationally ordered, abstract entities to attempt to explain anything in this fashion. This kind of philosophy, according to Comte, supported a legalistic social order, such as was found in feudal Europe. Whereas the society based on theological thought was marked by the presence of warriors, the society based on metaphysical thought had a predominance of lawyers.

The metaphysical stage of the mind was represented most importantly, for Comte, by Catholic theology, and he felt that, during his lifetime, the mind was finding its way out of this form of thought and entering the positive or scientific stage. Although the positive form of philosophy had been developing for some time, there were, in Comte's view, too many features of metaphysical, Catholic thought remaining to solidly support the new industrial social order which should have, as its most suitable basis, the positive philosophy.

Comte rejected the search for causes, whether first, final, efficient or material, and preferred the search for laws. In the search for laws, we discover observable regularities in phenomena and attempt to describe these regularities in the form of laws, mathematically expressed if possible. For example, the inverse square law describes what we can observe in phenomena of gravitation and attraction. This law describes what is familiar to us as the weight of bodies. It represents a positivist approach to knowledge. If, on the other hand, we began to argue about what weight and attraction *really* are, we would be engaging in metaphysics, in Comte's terms, and he was at pains to help rid the modern mind of this form of thought (Comte 1975: 75).

Thus, theological thought supports a militaristic society, metaphysical thought supports a legalistic one and, finally, a positive or scientific philosophy is the most natural support for an industrial society. According to Comte, these were three, quite distinct, stages because he could witness periods of disorganization and reorganization as the mind moved from one form of thought to another and as the form of society changed accordingly. Such was the period in which

Comte was writing. If we can find disorganization in our society, he argued, we can rest assured that there is disorganization in our form of thought or philosophy. More specifically, in his time, too many metaphysical elements (and even some theological ones) characterized the thought of the day to provide the proper intellectual and moral support for an industrial society.

Comte attributed the chaos and instability evident in his time to the existence of an incompletely formulated positive or scientific philosophy which suffered from the inclusion of too many metaphysical and theological features. He saw it as his task to correct this fault and thereby, he assumed, to establish a stable, durable, industrial social order. His law of the three-stage development undergirds the whole of his thought. The philosophical/theoretical side will be discussed next.

THE POSITIVE PHILOSOPHY

SINCE THE French Revolution had failed to establish a stable order based on Enlightenment principles, Comte attempted to shore up those principles which, he thought, could do the job. The reorganization of society required, above all, intellectual reform. He wanted to replace Catholicism with his positive philosophy.

Although many individual sciences, such as physics, chemistry, and biology, had been developing quite nicely, no one had yet synthesized the basic principles of these sciences into a coherent system of ideas. This system, including a new science of society and politics, would provide the intellectual and moral basis of the new order. Comte wanted to create a place for this new science which was to intervene in reforming society. While the human mind tended to evolve naturally toward a positive stage, Comte wanted to complete the transition with a revolution in philosophy. He wanted to articulate science's basic principles, synthesize them into a single coherent system, and, finally, apply them to human society. Comte coined the term "sociology" in 1838.

First of all, Comte stated that we are to give up the metaphysical search for first and final causes and instead look for invariable relations between things (regular patterns in phenomena). This scientific method thus involves:

1. the observation of facts with a preparatory theory;
2. experimentation (in sociology this would mean controlled observation);
3. comparison (of different societies); and
4. a historical method (recall Comte's interest in the intellectual basis of social evolution).

For Comte, all that we can think about is the phenomenal world (observable events). All the events in this world are governed by a set of scientifically discoverable, invariable, natural laws. He wanted to discover these laws and reduce them to a set of principles. Rational knowledge, accessible to science is thus, for Comte, a unified whole.

As concerns the examination of society, Comte divided this analysis into social statics and social dynamics. While dynamics (the theory of change and development) was, for Comte, the most interesting, he also insisted that statics (the functioning of a society and its parts as an organic whole) should not be overlooked. The units or levels of analysis in these projects were the individual, the family, the society, and the species (Comte, in typical nineteenth century European fashion was to specify that this meant primarily the white race).

The individual, for Comte, while not a unit of sociological analysis, has by nature a tendency to let the affective (emotional) faculties predominate over the intellectual. Although human nature consists, in part, of inherently social tendencies, the development of society depends on the stimulation, use, and extension of intellectual faculties. As civilization, in turn, begins to grow, the intellectual faculties are more stimulated and, hence, develop further.

Comte saw each member of the family, a truly social unit, as naturally subordinated to one another according to sex and age. Marriage had been modified but never overthrown, and Comte saw the equality of the sexes as incompatible with society. Men, for Comte, were intellectually superior, whereas women were morally superior.

Social organization beyond the family unit was seen by Comte as presenting some opposing tendencies. The cooperation entailed in the "appropriation of employments" (what Marx and Durkheim were later to call the division of labour) runs counter to the sympathy characteristic of family life. With growing specialization of function (occupation), it becomes more difficult to feel sympathy with those in occupations other than one's own. We live significantly different lives. We also, even as an entire race, become, at the same time, more "bound up" with one another. As we become more specialized in our manual or intellectual work, it is also expected that we will be more indifferent to human affairs in general.

Nonetheless, argues Comte, these tendencies to disintegration are made up for by a "tendency in all human society to spontaneous government." "[I]ntellectual and moral forces tend to ever increasing social authority" (Comte 1975: 277). Whereas the Enlightenment thinkers had despised collective authority, Comte, like the conservatives, saw government as a necessary and spontaneous development.

As far as dynamics are concerned, Comte believed that human social development was firmly rooted in those faculties which were characteristically human, primarily the intellectual faculty. Our most essential qualities as human beings will be manifested in the most highly developed civilization. Social development, based on the growth of intellect, leads to the primacy of the "preponderant powers of human existence" (Comte 1975: 279), namely to the development of the positive philosophy.

Although the thinking or "figuring out" which is done in the initial stages of our development would seem to have to do with "material cares," with (particularly productive) action on the environment, even the subsequent material advantage tends to have the effect of providing us with more free time for thought and excites our intellectual functions toward more intense thought about nature. Even theological explanation was seen by Comte as fitting with this scheme. Thus, civilization, itself rooted in our natural, intellectual faculties, improves those faculties.

As this civilization begins to develop, population becomes more concentrated, and this provides a stimulus to further intellectual and moral development. Thus, reason, although naturally a human faculty, becomes more and more influential in "the general conduct of man and society" (Comte 1975: 284). For Comte, the history of the mind governs the history of society. Even during the theological stage, a class had developed which could devote a good deal of its time to speculation. This indicates the necessity of the theological stage for human development. The advance to the positive stage meant an emphasis on observable laws over a search for "primary" causes. By employing a positive philosophy and the laws and principles thereby deduced, we can foresee and modify natural events (Comte 1975: 292).

The development of the intellect and society makes itself felt differently in different sciences. In general, the theological stage sparks the understanding, the metaphysical maintains "speculative activity on all subjects" (292), and the positive, or final stage, allows for the extraction of laws and general principles which can be applied to alter nature and society. We might, in our current state, have a positive science in some basic realms, a metaphysical understanding of some more complex ones, and only a theological understanding of the social realm.

It was Comte's ultimate aim to make sociology a positive science. He developed a hierarchy of sciences beginning with mathematics as the most fundamental and rising in order through astronomy, physics, chemistry, biology, and sociology. In reverse order, these sciences study phenomena from the most complex to the most basic.

THE POSITIVE POLITY

As STATED IN his initial work of 1822, Comte's long-range hope was to apply his thought to the reorganization of society. It was this notion of intervention in society which brought him disfavour, mainly from the scientific community. It was over this issue that Mill decided to withdraw his stipend form Comte, even though Comte's intention to intervene in social affairs was already clear in *The Positive Philosophy*.

For someone who believed that the problems of nineteenth century society were due to intellectual anarchy, that society was formed from ideas, the use of positive philosophy to reform society is not such a far-fetched notion. If he could bring about a consensus about basic ideas and rid positive thinking of its theological and metaphysical aspects, Comte thought that social instability could be eliminated. The positive philosophy, he thought, was rooted in nature itself so that universal principles derived from it could lead to a stable social order.

In the concluding chapter to Volume 1 of *The Positive Polity*, entitled "The Religion of Humanity," Comte summarizes this project:

> Love, then, is our principle; order our basis; and progress our end. Such ... is the essential character of the system of life that positivism offers for the definite acceptance of society, a system that regulates the whole course of our private and public existence by bringing feeling, reason, and activity into permanent harmony. (Comte 1975: 381)

The affective element of our nature (remember Madame de Vaux), social sympathy, is primarily responsible for this harmonizing effect. The mind, affection, and courage will all benefit from the acceptance and application of positivism. The position of women, the family, the working classes, the capitalists, and intellectual labour are to feel the refinement of positivism and the harmonizing effect of the religion of humanity. Politics and social institutions are to be revolutionized.

Like most religions, the religion of humanity is to have priests. There are, in Comte's scheme, one high priest, seven national chiefs, and 20,000 sociologist/priests to oversee educational and moral matters. Improvements would be devised by positivist intellect, but would maximize affective harmony. He hoped that his motto, "Order and Progress," would be spontaneously adopted.

HERBERT SPENCER (1820-1903)

SPENCER WAS THE only one of the nine children in his family to survive infancy. His father was a teacher of mathematics and science but, ironically, did not hold this institutional enterprise in very high esteem and, along with Spencer's uncle, taught the young Herbert at home. He thus received formal training only in mathematics and physics.

Given his scientific inclinations, he achieved a job as engineer for the London and Birmingham Railroad, eventually becoming its chief engineer but later resigning to edit a magazine called *The Economist*. His first major publication was an article in *The Nonconformist* entitled "The Proper Sphere of Government," a sphere which Spencer decided was extremely limited. His political viewpoint on such matters was what is referred to as "laissez-faire," essentially one of non-intervention. In his view, the adaptation of individuals, species, or societies to the environment is a natural process and should not, therefore, be interfered with.

This is a point of view characteristic of the science of biology and, indeed, Spencer took from biology the following claims or assumptions:

1. the critical attributes of individuals and collectivities emerge from competition either among individuals or between collective populations;

2. social evolution involves movement from undifferentiated structures to differentiated ones, marked by interrelated functions; and
3. the differences among individuals and social systems are a function of having to adapt to varying environmental conditions. Adaptation (to environmental conditions) and differentiation (growing complexity of parts and specialization of these parts) are thus important concepts in Spencer's view of human social development.

In fact, much of Spencer's thought is evolutionary in character. For Spencer, not only biological species or societies evolve, but all matter, being in its simplest forms highly unstable, tends to differentiate and become more complex. If this appears to be a somewhat puzzling notion, consider (perhaps you have seen something like this in a chemistry lab) a lump of highly pure sodium. It is normally kept in a closed container away from other elements or compounds because of its unstable, volatile nature. When exposed, the result (its combination with other elements, or tendency to differentiate and become more complex) is rather dramatic.

Spencer proposed a Theory of General Evolution, according to which matter passes from a relatively indefinite, incoherent homogeneity to a relatively definite, coherent heterogeneity (Spencer 1972: 71). Biological species tend to evolve in such a way as to become more complex (i.e. to differentiate internally, to have interrelated, specialized parts). As for individual species, so for superorganic entities like societies. Societies evolve by adapting internally and externally, and, in Spencer's scheme, there is an evolutionary continuum from militant to industrial societies. Militant societies, nearer to the beginning of the evolutionary process, were concerned primarily with issues of offense and defense. Industrial societies tend to be primarily concerned with the production of goods.

The evolution of species or societies, for Spencer, is ultimately a matter of the "survival of the fittest." Darwin's term for this notion is "natural selection", and he was later to suggest that he actually preferred Spencer's phrase. According to this notion, evolutionary processes filter out unfit species. The eventual outcome of this process, for Spencer, is a better, even morally perfect civilization. Since he viewed this outcome as the result of a natural process, he was adamant about his laissez-faire or non-intervention policy. Adaptation is key in this process; individuals or species should not, in his view, be helped in any way, lest a weak or unfit species continue to exist and thus weaken the whole. While species and societies evolved according to laws of their own, there is a supremely individualist assumption in Spencer's view. The perfection of civilization demands the perfection of the social atom, the individual human.

In thus suggesting that the natural process of adaptation should not be interfered with, Spencer was indicating that by means of this process the unfit, the poor, ignorant, or unhealthy, would be "weeded out." Competition would see to it that the unfit, just as in business, would die out. The function of the state in all of this is primarily to protect the terms of contracts. Everyone had to live up to their word in agreements. Spencer would not even allow the institution of a post office, let alone welfare or universal health care.

Spencer's laissez-faire individualism had special appeal to American capitalists, and his theories were more popular in the United States than in his native England. If one were at "the top," one might find it comforting to view this as a natural result of one's own superior qualities. The social and political viewpoint to which Spencer's theoretical views lead is called Social Darwinism. This position would become the justification for the dissemination of racist and otherwise pernicious doctrines such as eugenics, the active weeding out of particular kinds of persons (See Hofstadter 1955).

Perhaps the best way to summarize this chapter is by pointing out the similarities and differences between Comte and Spencer:

1. both Spencer and Comte believed that the universe is governed by understandable, invariable natural laws;

2. that the different branches of knowledge form a rational whole;
3. that positive methods should be used exclusively without any metaphysical speculation;
4. that social phenomena form an interdependent whole;
5. both developed theories of evolution and progress; and
6. each developed typologies (a comparative scheme using ideal forms) of types of society.

Spencer disagreed, however, with the following assertions of Comte:

1. that society passed through three distinct stages;
2. that causality was less important than relations of affinity;
3. that government can use sociology to intervene in society;
4. that the sciences developed in any particular order; and
5. that psychology was only a subdiscipline of biology.

Spencer thus emerges as more of an individualist, whereas Comte presents what is more of a combination of liberal individualist and conservative, collectivist notions and arguments.

All of this now sets the stage for our presentation of the "big three" classical, sociological theorists: Marx, Durkheim, and Weber. The Enlightenment, the Conservative Reaction, Comte, and Spencer initiated the basic terms employed in the subsequent discussion of the nature of human society. Liberal and conservative viewpoints both informed these concepts as they continued their development into the late nineteenth century.

2

Karl Marx
(1818-83)

THE THOUGHT of Marx, probably more than that of any other western thinker, is subject to one-sided interpretation and outright misrepresentation. This situation is not helped by the fact that his thought is opposed by many who, not having read much of it, find the popular, political connotations associated with his name and ideas unacceptable and equate it with many of his "Marxist" followers who represent equally interested stands on behalf of particular governments or political groups. His thought is without question the most fraught with controversy and opposing interpretation.

The young Marx entered his career after the bourgeois revolution, at a time when many struggled and hoped for a socialist revolution. In this context, the problems which beset the bourgeoisie, a lack of social harmony and a well-functioning economy, were taken up as their own by many thinkers. In France and Britain, where the bourgeois revolution had occurred, industrialization was well under way, but in Marx's Germany, which had not experienced such a revolution, it was only beginning. The state of Germany was reflected in its thought which presumed to be able to take a universal view and to reconcile opposition in thought only. Marx hoped to unite thought and action, theory and practice.

The young Marx, on the advice of his father, began the study of law, but he soon abandoned this career (although not his interest in it) for the discipline of philosophy. After completing his doctoral work on Epicurean and Democritian philosophies of nature, he very soon became embroiled in the philosophical/political debates of the day. In 1842 he became editor of a weekly called the *Rheinische Zeitung*

(*Rhine News*, an outlet for a radical group called the Young Hegelians, see below). He resigned his editorship of the paper under pressure from the authorities, who accused him of being a communist. Upon hearing this from the authorities, Marx decided it would be a good idea to find out exactly what that meant.

Between 1843 and 1845, he found out about communism as well as other views by doing a lot of reading while in exile in Brussels and Paris. In 1843, he wrote his *Critique of Hegel's Philosophy of Right*, a critique of G.W.F. Hegel and his followers, with whom Marx had been associated. In 1844, he completed his "Paris Manuscripts" (*Economic and Philosophical Manuscripts of 1844*), a continued critique of Hegelian thought inspired by his reading of many extant works on political economy. In 1845, he announced his transition from a critique of philosophy or consciousness to a critique of real conditions or political economy. He began this transition in a work with Frederick Engels entitled *The German Ideology*. Here, he decided to attend to real conditions rather than to a critique of problematic conceptions of them. His basic understanding of the development of human society was begun in this work.

Soon afterwards, there began in many parts of Europe a fundamental movement against conditions in European societies. Working people in many cities openly revolted against their oppressors in 1848. Marx and Engels wrote *The Communist Manifesto* as a rallying cry to help inspire the movement. But these insurrections failed, and Marx subsequently moved to England and returned to the "drawing board."

Two subsequent works, *Wage Labour and Capital* and *Contribution to the Critique of Political Economy*, signalled a long career devoted to analyzing the functioning of capitalist society; the critique of conditions had begun in earnest. In the *Grundrisse*, he outlined at length his approach to and sketches for this analysis and critique. The first volume of his magnum opus, *Capital*, appeared in 1867. In this text, he developed his theories of value and surplus value as the basic tools in understanding the operation of a capitalist society. Two subsequent volumes also appeared after being edited by Engels. In these, he continued a very detailed analysis of circulation, capital, and the crises which might befall such a set of social relations, given what he illustrated as their oppositional or contradictory character.

He also wrote a three volume work, *Theories of Surplus Value*, which was a series of commentaries on the work of others on this topic. Near the end of his life, he went back to a more general look at human social development by commenting on the anthropological work of four earlier ethnological writers in *The Ethnological Notebooks*.

Marx's philosophical studies took place in an intellectual climate dominated by the thought of G.W.F. Hegel and his followers. Hegelian thought, in many respects, proceeds from ideas found in Enlightenment and conservative thought, as well as in Comte. The Enlightenment's emphasis on reason, the conservatives' on tradition and culture, and that of Comte on the primacy of forms of thought can be seen in the development of German Idealism from Kant to Hegel. For Kant, however, Newton's science provided adequate evidence that permanent insight into the laws of nature had been achieved. Kant asked, "How was such insight into nature possible?" Nature does not provide any privileged access to its own operation. Fleeting perceptions of sense data flowing into our perceptual apparatus are important, but, he asked,"How is knowledge possible?" His answer was that the human mind provided necessary "categories" for sorting all this data into something like knowledge. Foremost among these categories were "space," "time," and "causality."

As German Idealism developed from Kant through to Hegel, we find the movement of spirit, mind, or culture taking place outside the human subject. Hegel's notion is that all of this *develops* and that it does so objectively. It is still idealism, but it is seen as a real movement in history. Whereas Comte had seen historical progress in terms of the development of mind, of ways of knowing the world, in Hegel's work, this notion acquires some new twists. For Hegel, reality, the world which we occupy, is not an altogether reasonable place. Unlike Comte, therefore, Hegel did not believe that any amount of hard, positivist thinking or analysis could make any ultimate sense of things. The world and its contents simply do not form a rational whole, at least not yet. The world is not particularly reasonable, for Hegel, because reason (mind, spirit) has not been adequately manifested in the world.

In fact, according to Hegel, our history is the story of the gradual historical realization or manifestation of reason or spirit in the world. "Spirit" (*Geist* in Hegel's German) does not have the supernatural connotations which the term "spirit" has in English. If we think of spirit in terms of "spirit of the times" or culture, we have something much closer to Hegel's meaning.

This spirit (world-spirit) was, in the view of Hegel and his followers, coming to realization during the period in which they lived. (Hegel was to say that he was his own time apprehended in thought.) Many of these people asked the question: Can we, in the current state of affairs, see perfectly reasonable conditions and realities emerging from the mists of our history? Does the current state of affairs in religion, the state and government, philosophy, and society represent a reasonable, understandable condition?

At issue here is the recognition of reason, wherever it may be found. For Hegel's followers, this boiled down to a question of the status of authority and tradition in any vision of a reasonable state of affairs. In other words, would this "reasonable state of affairs" entail a final solidification of already familiar traditions (religious thought, metaphysics, law) and authority (governments, monarchies, the Church) or would it, on the contrary, involve the final overcoming of these hindrances to the freedom of the human spirit?

Reason thus emerges as *the* contested concept among Hegel's followers. They questioned whether the current ideas and institutions represented an appropriate home for the human spirit: "Are we there yet?" In other words: Would a reasonable state of affairs involve the overcoming or the solidification and realization of authority and tradition? Of course, this question represents some of the central concerns of the Enlightenment, the Conservative Reaction, Comte, and Spencer. For most of them, however, the issue is one of how to adequately represent an already rational world. Only with Comte, do we find an inkling of the notion that we produce such a world.

Returning to Hegel's followers, the debate centred around the place of authority and tradition in the final resting place of reason. Did authority and tradition have to be overcome, or more firmly manifested? The battleground for this debate was religion.

For the Young (or left) Hegelians, religion had to be overcome; it represented the fetters or chains holding back the development of a true, appropriate home for the human type of being. For the Old (or right) Hegelians, religion was seen, rather, as the true moral bond of human beings in society. Authority and tradition, thus, were seen by the Old Hegelians as becoming more solid, realized, and manifest in the world as reason or spirit made its historical advance; the Young Hegelians viewed this movement of spirit as one which hastened ever more inexorably toward emancipation from religious illusion and (self-) deception. According to the Young Hegelians, if you rid the world of religious illusions, you remove the misery from people's real conditions. According to the Old Hegelians, if you maintain religious authority and tradition, you thereby provide the final cement that binds us together in a properly and reasonably human society.

In the early 1840s, Marx was enamoured of the Young Hegelian position. He also joined the battle against religion, the most hotly contested issue concerning the status of reason in this entire debate. But Marx soon became critical of the Hegelian position, whether held by the Young or Old Hegelians. In his view, both positions granted religion more influence than was justified, and he did not think that people's conditions could be remedied by changing their minds.

CRITIQUE OF THE CRITICS
OF CONSCIOUSNESS

ALTHOUGH THE Young and Old Hegelians disagreed as to whether religion represented the chains or true bonds of humans in society, they both saw it as operating in the same way, as fundamentally influential in human life. They disagreed primarily about whether the current state of this influence should be condemned or celebrated. Marx came to disagree with both concerning the status of religion as fundamentally substantial. Thus whereas the Young Hegelians proceeded to criticize religious consciousness as having substantially ill effects on the human condition, Marx began to see this criticism itself as insubstantial, as ill-conceived in its attempt to affect this very condition.

Marx addressed this issue in his [1843] *Contribution to The Critique of Hegel's Philosophy of Right*. In the introduction to this work, Marx's main target was Ludwig Feuerbach. Feuerbach, in *The Essence of Christianity*, had criticized religion as the self-alienation of "Man." Religion for Feuerbach, rather than being divinely inspired, was a human product in a process in which human consciousness alienated itself. In this process, argues Feuerbach, human beings succeeded in divesting themselves of some of their best qualities and made these the properties of God or gods. Although he did not believe that the human being is a god, Feuerbach thought that the solution to this process of alienation was to criticize the process in order to reclaim the best qualities of the human being. Whereas God was seen as knowing, loving, merciful, wrathful, and as possessing many other powerful qualities, humans were emiserated in the bargain and were seen a wretches, as being weak, sinful, ignorant. A powerful critique of religious consciousness was thus seen as necessary to end this deception. We must realize that *we* have created religion, and this realization was the necessary step toward ending a miserable condition, a condition for which the creation of religion was seen as primarily responsible.

Marx, although he saw much of this criticism as insightful, did not think that such critiques would do much to ameliorate the human condition. Many in Germany had been involved in this critical project, and Marx begins his 1843 work with the comment that this critique was nearly completed in Germany. He saw the critique of religion as "the premise of all criticism" (Marx 1978:53). In the search for the divine, in the human attempt to find a better life, humans sought what they thought was God but found what was really only their own "reflection." Their own best human qualities were made out to be the perfected qualities of God.

The critique of this religious form of consciousness was, for Marx, inadequate. The existence of earthly, everyday misery is not done away with once the religious excuse for it has been refuted or criticized. This, for Marx, was the mistaken assumption of the Young Hegelians. Where Feuerbach had claimed, "Man makes religion; religion does not make man," Marx thought that this claim was all too abstract and ahistorical. It may be the basis of a critique of religion in general; it suggests that when people do not have a "home" appropriate to their "true, human essence," they tend to think of themselves in a religious way, as pale in comparison to gods. But, for Marx, the everyday, human world is fundamental, not religious conceptions of it, right or wrong. In other words, people live in such a world, such a set of social conditions, that religion or religious consciousness tends to become the way we think of ourselves. There is a relation between the world we live in and the way we think of this world. If, from a critical point of view, people seem to have a curious or in some way inadequate way of thinking about themselves and their world, then this may have something to do with the very conditions of that world. If something is inadequate about our ideas about our world, something may well be "inadequate" about that world itself.

For Marx, "[r]eligion is the sigh of the oppressed creature, the sentiment of a heartless world, and the soul of soulless conditions. It is the *opium* of the people" (Marx 1978:54). This last sentence is a very famous quotation from

Marx. One may be tempted to read this as a condemnation of religion in the sense that religious fantasies or illusions produce misery. We might think that the "opium" is *the* problem. Recall, however, that Marx has already suggested that religion is not fundamentally substantial, not a primary force, in this process. If we think of opium use as a response (perhaps not the wisest one) to misery, we have something closer to Marx's point. Religion, like opium, is something to which people may resort when other things (our actual, real lives) are amiss.

Thus when Feuerbach claimed that "man" makes religion, he was being far too abstract. Particular people, living under particular kinds of conditions, produce particular kinds of ideas, religious or otherwise, about these conditions. The Young Hegelians urged people to give up religious illusions about themselves and their world. For Marx, what is at issue is the necessity of changing the conditions which make illusions of various sorts necessary.

> The abolition of religion as the *illusory* happiness of men, is a demand for their real happiness. The call to abandon their illusions about their condition is a *call to abandon a condition which requires illusions*. The criticism of religion is, therefore, *the embryonic criticism of this vale of tears* [earthly life] of which religion is the *halo*. (Marx 1978:54)

In other words, we must begin to criticize earthly life, not only its religious reflection. Religion may cover up or camouflage a miserable condition, but the task of removing the camouflage to reveal the misery is only a beginning. The task is hardly completed by changing our consciousness.

In *The German Ideology*, written with his friend, Frederick Engels, Marx began the transition from a critique of (the critique of) consciousness to a critique of real conditions. This work begins with a continuation of his critique of the Young Hegelians, in general, and of Feuerbach, in particular. The Young Hegelians had been making some rather sweeping claims on behalf of the revolutionary effect and status of their work. Here, Marx facetiously commented that the Young Hegelians boldly claimed for themselves that they had repaired, merely by their writings, several centuries of historical troubles. Because of the nature of these exaggerated claims for intellectual work, Marx was to call them "heroes of the mind." All their activities had taken place in the realm of pure thought.

But what had they actually done? The Young Hegelians took encouragement from the fact that religion consisted of "mere phrases." For Marx, however, the Young Hegelians had succeeded simply in fighting mere phrases with more phrases. The relation between consciousness or thought and the reality which the thought or consciousness is about had not been thoroughly considered. What, for example, was the relation between German reality and Young Hegelian thought?

FROM THE CRITIQUE OF CONSCIOUSNESS TO THE CRITIQUE OF POLITICAL ECONOMY

UP TO this point, Marx had been engaged in critiquing others' critiques and had found them lacking. He now changed his focus from this critique of consciousness to a hard look at real conditions themselves. He suggested beginning with *real* premises. By this he did not mean that he had some special philosophical insight into the truest assumptions. His intention, rather, was to begin with real, living, human individuals. We must look at people, their conditions, their activity, and their relation to the rest of nature. What is characteristic of human beings is that, collectively, they have been able to alter the conditions in which they live and thereby actually produce their life. In Marx's words:

> Men can be distinguished from animals by consciousness, by religion or anything else you like.

> They themselves begin to distinguish themselves from animals as soon as they begin to *produce* their means of subsistence, a step which is conditioned by their physical organisation. By producing their means of subsistence men are indirectly producing their actual material life. (Marx 1978:150)

Most importantly, this condition means that it is possible for us to have a history. Various aspects of our human, collective existence grow, change, and develop. Once our relation with nature begins to be socially organized, the possibility exists for this relation to take different forms. History is the product of the tension between two distinctively human sets of relations: our relation with nature, how we work and produce with respect to the natural materials which are necessary for making the things we need; and the relations in society in which we are organized to carry out all our practical activity. These two sets of relations have a mutual influence on one another. The way in which we are organized in society has an effect on the way we "go to work" on nature and its materials, and the way we do this work (the way we are related to nature), in turn, has had an effect on the way we are related to one another in society.

Thus, we have a history. The way we do things, the way we live, can take on different social forms. Animals of a given species, say bears, tend to be pretty well the same the world over and have remained the same for an extremely long period of their existence on earth. A black bear in Canada and a black bear in Russia tend to have pretty much the same life. But the case is not so with people, certainly not in all periods of history. Marx's criticism of Feuerbach's statement about "man" making religion now becomes a little more meaningful. This statement is too abstract because there is no such thing as humans in general making religion in general. Particular peoples make particular religions due to particular, complicated, unique sets of conditions and relations. People in ancient India, for example, made Hinduism; people in early modern Europe made Protestantism. Feuerbach's formulation does not allow us to specify the differences.

Marx thus suggests allegiance to a principle of historical specificity. If we are interested in knowing about a particular people, we must pay attention to the detailed, highly-nuanced conditions in which those people lived, particularly the way in which they produced for themselves. When we engage in a particular form of practical, productive activity, we not only produce the goods necessary to sustain life, pure and simple, we also *re*produce the social form in which we perform all this activity. The way we live, think, and act is thus circumscribed in important ways by the way we produce and reproduce our lives. If we want to understand a people's law, religion, philosophy, literature, or science, we should first of all, according to Marx, become intimately familiar with the way they produce for themselves, with the conditions of their existence.

Marx's criticism of the Young Hegelians' critique of religion thus becomes clearer. There is a relationship between the relations and conditions of real life, on the one hand, and thought, belief, and law on the other. Finding fault with the thought or belief does nothing to correct the conditions which engender the thought. People produce their ideas, but they do this while they are being influenced by the practical aspects of life. There is no formula for deriving such a relationship, but if we want to understand people's consciousness, we must understand their productive life and relations in all of their details.

As people began to produce their means of subsistence, this production gave rise to specific sets of relations in society. At first, these relations were probably not very complex or (to put it in terms discussed earlier) there was not much internal differentiation. People's production was just enough to feed, clothe, and shelter the community's members. Of course, humans being rather intelligent and hard-working, they began to get better at these activities and were eventually able to produce more than the community could readily consume. This is what is known as developing a surplus product. What is done with this surplus? Is it stored, redistributed, allowed to rot, given to another community, or offered to the gods?

The existence of a surplus made it possible for classes to develop. In other words, the possibility was now present for some to own or decide the fate of the surplus, while for others, this possibility did not exist. Thus, the division of labour, classes, and the state emerged. Some hunted, others did not, some "owned" more goods than others, and some were ascribed positions of authority in the community. Society thus, according to Marx, went through a progressive development of successive divisions.

Once we have a history, and this history consists of the development of different social forms and sets of relations in which we produce for ourselves, it becomes possible to divide this history up into different, rather distinct periods, according to the fundamental kinds of relations existing in society at each stage of its development. The fundamental relation, for Marx, is that some own and others do not; some produce and others do not. Initially, Marx referred to these distinguishable forms as "forms of ownership," from tribal through ancient-communal to feudal. He later refined this scheme and called the distinct periods and their sets of relations "modes of production." European expansion and colonialism provided Marx with a glimpse of different societies and their histories.

As a surplus was produced and the division of labour became more complex, specific kinds of class relations developed. Whereas many other commentators had attempted to specify what was necessary for any and all production, Marx thought it much more important to identify the differences between different "modes of production." In this way production is seen as having a history, and we can emphasize, in our analysis, the *development* of these different forms. If we do not keep in mind Marx's emphasis on historical specificity, as noted above, we are in danger of committing errors similar to those committed by Feuerbach when he discussed "religion in general." If, for example, we find it curious that the Babylonians did not have investment banks or that the medieval Europeans did not organize the production of crops for profit, then we have utterly failed to understand the actual conduct of life in these societies.

In all modes of production, there is a class of non-producing owners and another class of non-owning producers. Those who do the work are not typically those who end up owning the products of that labour and, conversely, those who own the products are not typically those who have produced them. But this is not historically specific. This kind of relation has existed in very distinct ways, and it is the differences which were important for Marx in his understanding of history and of human social development.

Those who perform the labour in each period are bound, or unfree. While this is true for all periods, it was important for Marx to identify the specific way in which direct producers are bound. Marx refers to this specific way as "the social form of labour." Each mode of production has a fundamental class relation in which the direct producers are uniquely bound, and the differences between these social forms of labour were important to Marx for understanding development. The relation between owners and producers needs to be historically specified.

The earliest mode of production which Marx attempted to identify was called the Asiatic mode of production. This is currently the most hotly contested of the modes which Marx labelled. He identified it as a situation in which people laboured in village communities on state lands and paid a rent/tax to a state tax collector. Ancient China and India are examples. Some modern commentators object to the name because they consider this mode as characterictic of Mayan society as well as of Asian societies. Labour, according to those who subscribe to this mode, was bound to the village by custom and habit. Some others, however, suggest that this mode is really a form of another mode called the feudal mode of production. We shall make no attempt to settle this debate here.

The second mode which Marx identified is called the mode of production of Classical Antiquity. In this mode of production the basic relation was that between master and slave. Slavery, therefore, was the social form of labour found in this mode of production. The slave was bound to the person of the master. The master could dispose of the slave as he wished. Household production, for example in ancient Greece, Rome, or Egypt, was performed primarily by slaves. Of course, there were others in these societies, such as artisans and merchants, but most production was carried out by slaves, considered non-persons in this situation.

The third mode identified by Marx is called the feudal mode of production as exemplified by medieval European societies. The basic relation in these societies was that between lord and serf; therefore, the social form of labour was serfdom. It is most important to distinguish this from slavery. Whereas the slave was bound to the person of the master, bondage of this kind did not exist in feudalism. The serf, rather, was bound to the land by written law. If, for example, an estate changed hands, the serfs stayed on the land, not with their former lord. Complex legal arrangements characterized the formal relations between persons of different types in medieval European societies. A person's rights under the law depended on his/her formal status in this regard. Whereas ancient society tended to be urban in many respects, feudal estates were located in the countryside where the serfs carried out the most fundamental productive activities. There were merchants and artisans in the towns, but the lord/serf relation characterized this kind of society.

Finally, we come to the mode of production still common today, the capitalist one. This mode is characterized by the fundamental relation of capitalist/wage labourer. The social form of labour is wage labour and the wage labourer is formally free. This freedom, however, has no substance to it. The labourer is free to sell his/her labour to the highest bidder on the market but, of course, must do this, if s/he is to survive. Some have called this freedom the freedom of both rich and poor to sleep under bridges if they wish. In any case, the wage labourer is not bound in any formal way.

THE ANALYSIS OF
CAPITALIST SOCIETY

In 1847, Marx gave a series of speeches on
the operation of capitalist society and later (1849) published
them in pamphlet form, entitled *Wage Labour and Capital*.
In this work, he covers, in brief, the important terms of his
analysis of capitalist society. Of primary importance in this
initial analysis is the relation (as the title suggests) between
wage labour and capital, both as concepts and as real persons in society whose qualities and features derive from that
relation. In other words, Marx argues that neither the wage
labourer nor the capitalist as such have properties or attributes which belong to them apart from this relation.
Similarly, capital, which could exist in the form of money,
raw materials, or physical plant, for example, is not capital
simply by virtue of being certain kinds of things. These kinds
of things are capital, he argues, only when they enter into a
particular kind of historically specific relation.

Wage labourers produce commodities, goods which are
produced for exchange. The commodities are sold on the
market, and the capitalist pays the labourer a wage. The
capitalist gives up some of his capital to the wage labourer
in the form of wages in return for the use of his/her labour-
power. Labour-power is thus itself a commodity; it is bought
and sold. The wage labourer gets a means of subsistence,
and the capitalist gets labour-power. How is its price determined? The main ingredient in this price, for Marx, is, as
with any commodity, its cost of production. In the case of
wage labour, this cost of production is means of subsistence:
food, shelter, and clothing. So the capitalist gives up a portion of the capital in the form of this means of subsistence in
exchange for the labour-power of the wage labourer.

There is competition in this process between buyers and
sellers; the wage labourer wants higher wages and the capitalist hopes to keep them down. There is also competition
between buyers for market share and for cheaper or more
skilled labour. Competition also exists between sellers; who

gets the higher paying job? Capital moves from one industry to another in order to maximize returns, and labour, too, must move and is often kept idle in pools of cheap, under-employed labour which Marx referred to as the reserve army of labour.

The capitalist, in all of this, is hoping to increase the exchange-value of the goods in his/her possession. This, after all, is the name of the game. The goods in possession of the capitalist, furthermore, are called capital when they enter into this kind of process. At first glance, it appears that they are all products of past labour; they are accumulated labour. But does this status as embodied, past labour make them capital? Marx's answer to this question is "no. The same kinds of objects, machines, money, raw materials of all sorts, have existed in previous societies but were not capital. In those societies, a portion of those goods was not given up as wages in exchange for labour-power with the result of increasing the exchange-value of the capitalist's possessions.

These things are capital, therefore, only when they enter into a social relation with wage labour thus having their value increased. This is a historically specific relation and cannot be deciphered by looking at the physical features of the objects considered. Marx uses an analogy to make this point. In a particular period in history, black people became slaves in quite large numbers. But is a black person a slave by virtue of being black? — Of course not. Only under a particular set of historically determined social circumstances did black persons become slaves. By analogy, a machine, for example, is capital only under a particular set of historically determined social conditions. Only when a portion of material is given up in the form of wages to increase the exchange-value of things are those things capital. What is characteristic of capital is that it increases its value. This can happen only in relation with wage labour, and this is the social relation of which Marx is speaking. Things become capital only in a particular social relation with wage labour. Capitalists and wage labourers must be in relation for this to happen.

In his 1859 *Contribution to the Critique of Political Economy*, Marx laid further groundwork for his analysis of capitalist society; he exhaustively sketched out the plan for this analysis in the *Grundrisse*, a work which was not intended for publication being, rather, his notes for the entire project. The introduction to this latter work is about the only place where we find Marx becoming explicitly methodological. Here he illustrates just how he thinks one ought to go about examining capitalist society. Whereas it may appear to make sense to begin with the most concrete features of such a society, such as the population as the foundation of production, Marx, however, suggests just the opposite: we must begin with the apparent results of the process and, in terms of the current political economic understanding of those results, work back to the concrete features. Thus, he begins with the concepts of value, money, commodities, and capital and proceeds to ferret out the problems entailed in the current usage and understanding engendered by those concepts.

THE LABOUR THEORY OF VALUE

IN HIS main work, *Capital*, Marx finally engages in a thorough analysis of the relations of capitalist society, and he does so by beginning precisely with the concepts of commodities, money, and value. In a capitalist society, he begins, wealth presents itself in a particular form, commodities. In all societies, people produce things which satisfy their wants and needs. The more things we have, the more cloth, the more gold, the more silos of corn, the wealthier we are. These things, however, are not commodities unless they get exchanged. People in a capitalist society live by exchange to acquire the things they need.

A commodity, therefore, whatever else it may be, is a good which satisfies some want or need. If we have a particular want, we attempt to acquire something which is capable of satisfying that want. We look for an item which we think will satisfy that need. If I am hungry, for example, I might look for a loaf of bread, rather than a pair of shoes (although in many university cafeterias it is often difficult to tell the difference). Thus the item which I acquire must be capable of satisfying this want by virtue of its natural properties. Bread is easier to chew and more nourishing than shoe leather. This is the case for all people, whatever kind of society they may live in.

All goods, whether commodities or not, have a use-value. The natural properties of a given kind of item make it useful for the purpose of satisfying particular needs or wants. They are, furthermore, the products of human labour. In order for the bread to satisfy my hunger and keep my body alive, in order for the shoes to keep my feet warm and dry, each must have been the product of a particular kind of labouring activity. To get bread, some milling and baking labour had to have been expended in its production. To get shoes, some shoemaking or cobbling labour had to have been done. In terms of the use-value of any item, therefore, it matters which particular kind of labour was expended in its production. Marx calls this labour "concrete labour." The use-value of a good or item, therefore, depends on the natural properties of the material and on the specific kind of concrete labour involved in its production.

In our kind of society, however, we acquire goods by exchanging them. We produce privately, rather than in some other arrangement, for example, where brothers-in-law produce food for their sisters' families, as in the Trobriand Islands. We now use money for this, but in an earlier form of our society, we would take a surplus of our own goods to market in order to acquire something we needed. If I were a baker, for example, and had an abundance of bread, but my feet were bare, I might well take some of my bread to market to exchange for a couple of pairs of shoes. Nothing has changed concerning the use-value of either the bread or the shoes. Natural properties and concrete labours are still the essential considerations in this regard.

As soon as a good is exchanged, however, it acquires another feature unrelated to its use-value, namely, exchange-value. When I take my bread to market, how is it determined how many loaves of bread I must give up in exchange for how many pairs of shoes? Current, commonsensical answers to this question might be such responses as: quality, supply and demand, or cost of production. While supply and demand may certainly affect price on any given day or week, Marx's answer is closer to the "cost of production" response. Quality, in his view, turns out to be intimately related to cost of production.

If, for example, over a relatively long period of time, say, several months, twenty-five loaves of bread seem consistently to exchange for two pairs of shoes, how is this quantitative relation determined? As soon as the bread or the shoes become, not simply humanly produced goods, but commodities, goods produced for exchange, they seem to acquire another property in addition to their ability to satisfy wants and needs by virtue of their natural properties. In what does this exchange-value consist? The ability of the shoes, by virtue of the properties of leather or of the effect of cobbling on leather, to keep my feet warm does not determine how many loaves of bread one must give up in exchange for them. The commodity's property of being exchangeable for other commodities has nothing to do with its natural properties.

How much of something else we may get in return for a certain amount of our own commodity does have to do with the cost of production of each. What do all these commodities have in common, so that they may be freely exchanged for one another? They are all products of labour, but how does this help us to answer the question? If it costs more to produce something, then it seems reasonable to expect more in exchange for it. What are these costs? Foremost among these costs, for Marx, is the time it takes to produce it. At a common-sense level, this is not a difficult notion to appreciate. I can buy a pen for forty-nine cents, or I can buy a better one for over a hundred dollars. One, of course, is a better quality pen than the other. Of what does this quality consist? One is made of plastic or of relatively cheap metal, and the other is made of more finely machined parts, some of which may even be gold-plated. I may always have wanted a really good pen and have gone out specifically to acquire the good pen. My desire, however, does not determine the fact that I must pay over a hundred dollars for it. While I am certainly getting a better quality pen in the process, this only begins to explain the difference in exchange-value.

When we consider all the elements of the more expensive item which make it one of better quality, the major component in all of them is time. It took time to do the machining with better instruments and tools; it took time to prospect for, mine, and smelt the gold. Exchange-value, therefore, seems to have to do with the consideration of *how much* labour is contained in the commodity, rather than with *what kind*. The kind of labour, concrete labour, has to do with the use-value of the commodity. The quantity of labour contained in it has to do with its exchange-value.

Remember, however, that each commodity is produced by a particular, concrete kind of labour. When considering the exchange-value of a commodity, it matters simply how much labour went into its production, not which kind. Marx calls this "labour expended without regard to the mode of its expenditure," or "*abstract labour.*" What determines the exchange-value of the commodity? Marx would answer: it is the amount of abstract labour, labour pure and simple, contained in it. But, of course, we cannot go out and actually perform anything like "abstract labour." We can perform baking, cobbling, mining, gardening, or any other concrete form of labour, but we cannot perform abstract labour.

Thus we "abstract from" the specific properties of the kind of labour which produced a commodity to determine how much abstract labour, labour expended without regard to the mode of its expenditure, there is in that commodity. Generally and in an intuitively commonsensical way, it is cogent to suggest that the longer it takes to produce something, the more is it worth, the more exchange-value it has. Now, if it takes me longer to make something, say, a table, I cannot thereby expect my table to be worth more than a similar table made in half the time. Exchange-value depends, not on the amount of time any individual takes to produce a given commodity, but rather on the "socially necessary labour time" typically taken to produce it. This is determined by the prevalent technology and intensity of labour in a given society at a given time.

But, what about this abstraction? This is in no way an intellectual, cognitive, or mental process. We do not actively and mentally "disregard" concrete properties and kinds of labour. The abstraction is a real, social process which occurs through acts of exchange. Consider the example of the bread and shoes. The bread has been produced in so many hours of baking; the shoes have been produced in a given number of hours of cobbling. The given proportion in which amounts of them are exchanged is *not* determined by equal numbers of hours having been expended in the actual production of the exchanged quantities of goods. If twenty-five loaves of bread exchange for two pairs of shoes, this does not mean that the same number of actual hours of labour were expended in the production of each. It does mean that the same amount of society's total labour *is* contained in each. This is a troubling complication which makes the entire process, as outlined by Marx, more difficult to grasp, but it is absolutely necessary to look at it in order to understand Marx's analysis.

In the above example, the reduction to hours of labour pure and simple is accomplished through the extended and continued process of exchange over relatively long periods of time. Bread and shoes, as well as a host of other commodities, are being exchanged on the market. Since levels of technology and the organization of the labour process can, of course, vary from one branch of production to another, we cannot simply equate numbers of hours actually spent in the production of different items. The reduction to abstract labour, hours of socially necessary labour time, is made without our knowledge in the acts of exchange themselves. When people satisfy wants and needs through the constant and continuous exchange of commodities, this constant exchange activity establishes proportions of exchange between given commodities according to the amount of society's total labour contained in them. No one has to be conscious of this; no cost accountant must figure it out with a pencil (or computer). It would be a completely intractable problem in any case.

In the act of exchange, baking, in our example, is being equated to cobbling. The equation between specific amounts of bread and shoes holds because the same amount of society's total labour is contained in each. The baking embodied in twenty-five loaves of bread and the cobbling contained in two pairs of shoes each represents the same amount of abstract labour, hours of socially necessary time, of labour pure and simple. Value, thus, is something social. One cannot inspect any commodity with a microscope or in a chemistry lab and expect to find or distill out the exchange-value. The value of a commodity, which is only ever manifested in the form of exchange-value, is a feature of goods when they occur in a particular kind of society, a society in which people supply wants and needs by producing goods for exchange.

The commodity, therefore, is a two-fold thing. It has a use-value and, as such, has a particular set of natural properties determined in part by the specific kind of labour performed in its production. Use-value is thus determined by the natural properties of the materials out of which the commodity is made and by the form of concrete labour expended in its production. Exchange-value, on the other hand, has nothing to do with the natural properties of any commodity. Whereas the use-value of a commodity can be seen as answering the question, "What is this good for?", the exchange-value of the same commodity might be seen as representing an answer to the question, "How much of something else can I get for this?" This question is answered, in Marx's analysis, in terms of amounts of total social labour, hours of socially necessary labour time, amounts of abstract labour.

All of this occurs, and is made possible, by the fact that we live in a society in which people privately produce commodities for exchange and satisfy needs by exchange. The predominance of satisfying needs and wants in this way is a relatively recent development. The "two-fold nature of the labour embodied in the commodity" (which Marx considered to be his contribution to this analysis) occurs because of this arrangement in society.

Thus exchange-value, as opposed to use-value, emerges as a social property of goods when people satisfy wants and needs by exchanging the products of labour, rather than distributing them in some other way. As a constituent part of the goods, its existence depends on a particular historical form of the division of labour, one in which private producers exchange products. In the world of commodities, we have social relations between things. Producers are related to one another through their products; hence, we have material relations between persons.

When we view the action of commodities on the market, the quantitative relations between them appear accidental. All the commodities produced can be exchanged. Thus, 20 yds. linen = 1 coat = 1.5 oz. gold = 5 bushels wheat = *etc.* It is this which makes it difficult, according to Marx, to decipher the basis of exchange-value in abstract labour. Now, of course, we use money for this. This simply means that a particular commodity has emerged as the universal equivalent, as the kind of good which proves adaptable to this purpose. For the purpose of exchanging for other things which we need, it is more convenient to carry silver in our pockets than it is to carry cows or iron.

In the expression 20 yds. linen = 1 coat, we are told that the same quantity of society's labour, labour pure and simple, is embodied in each. If, however, a new sewing machine makes it possible to produce coats in half the time, the quantities in our expression will change. Now, 10 yds. linen = 1 coat. Even though we can now have more coats, an increase in material wealth, this increased quantity of coats may represent a decrease in value. For Marx, "[t]his antagonistic movement has its origin in the two-fold character of labour" (1978: 312).

Since technology and the organization of labour processes are constantly altering the productivity of labour in its different branches, the proportions in which commodities are exchanged are also changing. Because of this, the exchange-value of commodities appears to be rather accidental or driven purely by market forces. Adam Smith, for example, suggests, with the use of his notion "the invisible hand," that the market takes care of itself harmoniously. Marx takes issue with such notions. In Marx's example of 20 yds. linen

= 1 coat, we can see the effect, for example, of a new sewing machine on the proportion in which these two commodities are exchanged. Amounts of weaving are being compared to amounts of tailoring, and these amounts, expressed as quantities of labour pure and simple, are found to represent equal parts of society's total labour. All this is the case only because products get exchanged.

To continue with this example, the linen stands in the relative form of value. It is having its value expressed. If, for example, we are the owner of the linen, we take it to the market in hopes of exchanging it for something else which we need, say, a coat. We are thus asking about the linen, "How much of something else is it worth?" We are asking about its exchange-value. At the same time, we are inquiring about the use-value of the coat. We are interested in the ability of the coat to keep us warm. We are interested in how many coats or how good a coat we can get for how much linen. The coat here stands in the equivalent form of value.

The equivalence in this relation expresses the fact that the same amount of abstract labour, the same fraction of society's total labour, is contained on either side. Weaving and tailoring are considered the same, as far as value is concerned. When it comes to use-value, however, tailoring is specifically what we are after, if it is a coat that we want. We are interested in a social property of our linen, its exchange-value. We are interested in a natural property of the coat, its use-value. A curious fact thus arises in consideration of this equivalent form. A social property (exchange-value) is expressed in a natural property (use-value),and abstract labour is compared to concrete labour. The exchange-value of the linen is expressed, but the form in which this is expressed is use-value, a natural property. Thus, to the casual observer, it appears as though exchange-value might be a natural property of the commodity.

THE FETISHISM
OF COMMODITIES

THE PECULIARITIES of the equivalent form of value outlined briefly above indicate why it is that exchange-value might appear to be a natural property of a commodity; the exchange-value of one commodity is expressed in terms of the use-value, a natural property, of another. Thus Marx's theory of the relations of a capitalist society is also a theory of why those relations are not readily visible to members. In this form of society, we have social relations between things and material relations between persons. This is due to a particular historical development of the social division of labour. The features of our lives and relations take on the appearance of something natural, as permanent or fixed features of the things, our products, through which we are related.

Marx called this phenomenon, the fetishism of commodities, and borrowed the term "fetishism" from the early French anthropologist, Charles de Brosses. De Brosses used "fetish" to describe certain features of animistic religions. In some cultures, belief systems are marked by the attribution of demons or spirits to many objects of the world. Also in these cultures, members, according to such beliefs, must behave toward these objects/spirits in appropriate ways in order to keep the world in order and to avoid harm to themselves and their group. In de Brosses' Eurocentric view, this is a fetish. These people are controlled by their own mental products, their own ideas.

Marx believed that people in our kind of society are also controlled by their products. In this case they are controlled by their physical products, the products of their material interchange with nature. The "action" in such a society appears to be in the world of things. The world of commodities is one in which the relations between things appear to determine the fate of persons; this fate seems also to have something to do with the natural properties of those things. "[T]he social character of men's labour," the exchange-value of a commodity, "appears to them as an objective character stamped upon the product of that labour" (Marx 1978: 320). For Marx, of course, the "bottom line" in all of this is the particular relations found in that form of society. The appearance, however, is otherwise: "There it is a definite social relation between men, that assumes, in their eyes, the fantastic form of a relation between things" (Marx 1978: 321). Things, thus, appear to rule people, and, from another perspective, this is exactly the case. Things *do* rule people, but not by virtue of their natural properties; rather, they do this by virtue of the relations between people in society. That value is something social is difficult to perceive, and this difficulty is the result of the relations in society which produce value. Because we are dealing with things, it is tempting to see their action as something natural.

In everyday terms, we hear examples of this confusion quite often. The TV financial news or newspaper financial pages report on the action of things. "What is gold doing?" "What are soy beans doing?" These are the kinds of questions which we might hear if we get close to commodities or stock brokers. Their zealous reading of the financial pages informs their buying decisions. This is not a fantasy; their ken in such matters far exceeds that of the average sociological theorist. If I had any money, I would ask them, not Marx, where to invest it. The object of such knowledge, however, is not a natural property of things. Marx, while not a very skilled investment broker, was a more thorough analyst of the social basis for such action on the market. That we are ruled by our products, is attributable to the fact that most of us do not own them. Most of us have only one commodity to sell, our labour-power. This, for Marx, indicates an exploitative, class relation.

SURPLUS VALUE

The serf in a feudal society was exploited but s/he was not confused about this. Serfs worked a small piece of land to support their own families; they worked on the lord's lands and on his roads. They "owned" their own means of production. Most of them had very hard lives; a few were not so badly off.

In the towns of medieval Europe, we find some burghers administering the towns (hence the German term "Burger" (citizen) or the French "bourgeois"), as well as artisans and merchants. As feudalism began to wane, many serfs wanted to escape to the towns (there is freedom in town air). They might have gone to work for an artisan and, if lucky, become an apprentice. Merchants would sell the artisans' products in far away markets (other towns).

As feudalism declined, however, the way of life of the towns began to spread. At first, a system referred to as "mercantilism" emerged. Some merchants were able to become quite wealthy simply by buying up the wares of local artisans and transporting them long distances to places where they could fetch a high price for them. They would also bring back items which were not locally available, such as silk from China. In the northern Italian cities of Genoa, Venice, and Pisa, for example, many merchants flourished toward the end of the middle ages.

The next step in this process was for the merchant to gain control over the production of the goods which he was selling abroad. At first, this led to a "putting-out system" or "cottage industry." In the production of a given kind of item, say, woollen cloth, the putter-out/merchant would buy wool from a farmer, take it to someone else to be washed, then elsewhere to be dyed, carded, spun, and, finally, woven. Each of the operatives at the different stages of the process would probably be supplementing their farm incomes, and the whole family would sometimes take part in aspects of this production.

Ultimately, there developed putters-out who would sell to merchants, and these "industrialists" eventually organized the production, or at least as many aspects of the process as possible, under one roof. This centralization necessitated the hiring of wage labour on a large scale. But most potential workers were still located in the countryside. When these people were "freed" from the land, they went to work in the new industries in the cities. Freed from their means of production, they had little choice but to make their living in this way. They had only one commodity to sell, their labour-power.

In the above description of the labour theory of value, we have been outlining processes germane to a state of affairs called simple commodity production. This is a condition where many people are independent, small producers who own the products of their labour and sell these products for the other things they need. As a pure and predominant form of production, this state of affairs probably did not exist for very long. Of course, now we know that most of us do not live by selling the products of our labour. We sell our labour-power.

Above, we describe how labour-power becomes a commodity; however, labour-power as a commodity has existed for a very long time. The Babylonians had wage labour. But the dominance of labour-power as a commodity is fairly recent, and its rise to dominance probably began around the sixteenth century in Europe. Since labour-power is a commodity, like other commodities, it has a use-value and an exchange-value. Its exchange-value, as discussed above, is essentially its cost of production. In other words, how much does it cost to keep wage labourers as a class alive? The answer, of course, is the cost of food, shelter, and clothing. The capitalist gives up a portion of capital in the form of these necessities, and this results in the payment of wages. There are other forms of non-waged labour, such as domestic, not considered in this analysis.

But what is the use-value of labour-power? Why does the capitalist buy it? As we learned in the section above on *Wage Labour and Capital*, the answer to this question is to increase the exchange-value of his/her goods (i.e. for profit).

The capitalist, after all, is not in business for fun. The capitalist goes to the market to buy labour-power. What is contracted, for this bargain, whether formally written or not, is for the wage labourer to work for the capitalist for a certain number of hours per day in return for a wage, approximately equal to the labourer's cost of living. So the wage labourer, say a weaver, comes to work for the capitalist and agrees to work fourteen hours a day in return for three shillings, the approximate daily cost of production of labour-power in England in 1867. With this, the labourer could rent a garret room, buy enough bread to sustain life, secure minimal clothing, and occasionally go to the public house for a pint.

What is the capitalist receiving in exchange? For the three shillings, the capitalist is getting fourteen hours of labour. During this fourteen hours, the labourer is producing cloth. However if, for example, it takes the labourer eight hours to produce enough cloth, which when sold is equivalent to the wages or the three shillings, s/he does not get to go home (nor to the public house). S/he must, according to the contract, keep working for an additional six hours. The cloth produced during this period, when sold, accrues to the capitalist in the form of *surplus value*, profit (these are not the same; see below).

The first eight hours mentioned above, necessary labour time, is that period during which the labourer works to cover the wage contract. The remaining six hours, surplus labour time, is that period during which the labourer's products increase the exchange-value of the capitalist's goods. This, after all, is the use-value of labour-power, its capacity to create value.

Now the capitalist, anxious to further increase the exchange-value of the goods, will attempt to further enhance this process. The first and most obvious way to do this is to increase the absolute length of the working day. It still costs only three shillings to produce labour-power, but now, if the working day is increased by two hours to a total of sixteen hours, the surplus labour time is increased from six to eight hours, two more hours in which the labourer's products help to enrich the capitalist. This represents an increase in *absolute surplus value*.

There has proven to be a high political and social cost to this strategy, however. Labour movements against this kind of practice proved costly to the capitalist. As the labourers' health and quality of life declined, they became unwilling to accept this way of increasing surplus value. There emerged another way of increasing surplus labour time which did not require lengthening the working day. This strategy involved changing the relative lengths of the necessary and surplus periods of the day. If that portion of the working day devoted to necessary labour time could be reduced, then the remaining period would be increased. In other words, if a way could be found for the workers to produce enough to cover the wage contract in less time, more surplus value would accrue to the capitalist. By speeding up production, introducing new technologies, reorganizing the labour process, and by cheapening the means of life (food, shelter, and clothing), the capitalist proved capable of changing the relative lengths of the parts of the working day. If the necessary labour time is reduced to six hours, and the length of the whole working day remains at fourteen hours, the surplus labour time is increased from six to eight hours, an increase in surplus value for the capitalist. This represents an increase in *relative surplus value*.

CAPITAL, CONTRADICTION, CRISIS AND STATE

ALTHOUGH VALUE, money, commodities, and exchange are, indeed, central concepts in Marx's analysis of modern society, each of these refers to entities or practices which existed long before the advent of capitalist society. The rise to dominance of money and commodities is a large part of the story but, as one may expect, it is the emergence of capital which decisively marks off capitalist society from its predecessor. As described in Marx's brief work, *Wage Labour and Capital,* capital can appear in many forms such as money, raw materials, and machines. What makes each of them capital is its place in a set of conditions and relations which result in ever-increasing value appropriated by a capitalist class. This has been the case for about 400 years. In fact, recent coining of the term "globalization," notwithstanding, "[t]he modern history of capital dates from the creation in the sixteenth century of a world-embracing commerce and a world-embracing market" (Marx n.d.: 145).

The widening exchange of commodities and the rise to dominance of a money economy, each of which encouraged the other, set the stage for the emergence of capital in its first form, money, which may exist simply as money, or as capital. When money is capital it participates in a different form of circulation. A peasant, for example, may sell grain to buy clothes. Marx's shorthand representation of this sequence is C-M-C; a commodity (grain in the example) is exchanged for money which is, in turn, exchanged for a commodity (clothes). Items of equal value are exchanged in each case, and the recipient of each commodity gains a use-value and has used his/her own labour-time (cultivating, sewing, etc.) efficiently. Few people, even in the sixteenth century, were capable of the efficient production of everything they needed.

Money emerges as capital when, rather than satisfying a specific need or want, the circulation sequence has an increment of exchange-value as its aim. The sequence M-C-M' (buying a commodity with money in order to sell it or a transformation of it for more money) represents buying in order to sell, whereas our exemplary peasant has sold in order to buy. In this sequence, buying in order to sell (M-C-M'), money is converted into more money (value is added) only if the initial money purchases a commodity. The original money becomes capital only by dint of this apparently mysterious value-adding process in which something must happen to the commodity in the meantime, even if this is merely to transport it to a relatively distant location where it may be sold for a higher price. Money, in this case, emerges as merchants' capital. So capital can be money, and capital can be commodities; somehow, in changing form, value also changes magnitude. M-C-M' is thus the general formula for capital.

In the exchange of equivalents, remember, items of equal value are being exchanged. The same portion of society's labour is embodied in both sides of an act of exchange. Even if someone is being swindled, the same total value exists in the world of exchanged goods. (Marx n.d.: 159) Surplus value, an increment in the magnitude of value, cannot have its origin in the process of circulation. How do we move from the exchange of equivalents, our starting point, to an explanation of added value? Although the general formula for capital, M-C-M', certainly appears to reflect adequately the state of affairs in either mercantilism or modern industry (value does increase in the process), the formula at the same time opposes or contradicts the rule of equivalence of exchange which is its basis.

The capitalist who advances (invests) a good part of the material in his/her possession for production sells the commodities produced at their value (or even below it, see below); yet, the process yields a surplus value and the capitalist is its owner. This capitalist realizes part of this surplus value as profit, while the rest of it may be realized by others as interest, merchants' profit, and rent.

The M-C-M' process must continue if the capitalist is to remain a capitalist. In order for the sequence to continue, a portion of the returns must be converted into means of production. Marx calls this "capitalist reproduction." Surplus value realized as profit in the form of money must be used to purchase more means of production if it is to function as capital (i.e. to have its value increased). To function as capital, furthermore, some of it must be spent in the purchase of labour-power, since it is labour which converts means of production into commodities. Once this is grasped as a class relation (capitalists purchasing the labour-power of wage labourers), claims Marx, the mysterious power of money to increase in value disappears.

Initial capital advanced must be replenished, and labour-power must be purchased for an additional period. Labourers receive means of subsistence as wages which are a part of the value of their past products. Initial capital is reproduced; to continue to operate *as* capital, it must function in continued relation with living labour. Where all means of production are appropriated by a given class, others are forced to sell their labour-power. Even if the very first bit of capital was accumulated by the employer, surplus value becomes, in Marx's words, "value appropriated without an equivalent" (n.d.: 535). As soon as that initial capital functions as such by exchanging part of itself for labour-power, the unpaid labour of others is materialized in commodities of increased value.

In Marx's view, it is this unpaid labour which produces the increase in value, whereas other political economists had attempted to locate its source in the nature of circulation or of money. Capitalist production begins when the labourer class must sell its labour-power and, thus, is separated from the means of production. Capitalists gain wealth, while wage labourers produce capital and reproduce their own dependence on this alienated wealth for subsistence. "This incessant reproduction, this perpetuation of the labourer is the sine qua non of capitalist production" (Marx n.d.: 536). Labour-power is reproduced as is the means of production. Marx's identification of this source of wealth and added value is most important. He is concerned not simply to correct a few subtle errors in the manuals which instruct the capitalist about how to get rich; they can do that without any help from him. He is at pains to point out the fundamental importance of wage labour, and its relation to capital as the source both of wealth and of the power of the state to maintain this relation. The activity of wage labourers produces wealth and value and reproduces the social and political relations in which such value is produced. It appears that this is voluntary due, according to Marx, to the *fictio juris* (legal fiction) of the contract. The Enlightenment assumption of the meeting of autonomous and independent minds as fundamental entities called "persons" (the legal fiction) in the marketplace receives a blow at the hand of Marx, who in other respects is something of a child of the Enlightenment (rational and scientific in his approach to the forces of production, and a proponent of the notion that many current political concepts are religious in character).

Recall the discussion of absolute and relative surplus value as noted above. The wage-contract is for an entire working day (whatever its length), and the necessary labour-time is shorter than this; otherwise, capitalist relations are not reproduced. The fact that employers and workers can change their particular individual relations by changing jobs creates the appearance of a voluntary contract, but when the groups are viewed as classes, the legal fiction appears as just that. The class of social labour, since it has been "freed" from the means of production, must sell its labour-power in order to survive.

Capital, the form of wealth and power in a capitalist society, is accumulated (produced and reproduced) on an increasing scale. "Employing surplus value as capital, reconverting it into capital, is called accumulation of capital" (n.d.: 543). Without this conversion, capital does not accumulate, and without accumulation, the M-C-M' process grinds to a halt; there must be more "C" to be transformed by more labour so that "M'" may continue to result.

To accomplish what Marx calls "simple reproduction," some of the surplus value produced in the production process must be converted into additional means of production and subsistence (wages) for wage labour. The purchase of additional labour to work on more means of production (above that which replenishes the initial means advanced by the capitalist) completes the conversion of surplus value into capital. Where, for example, an original capital of $10,000 was the product of the capitalist's family's labour, all additional capital is owing to the unpaid portion of labour-power employed in subsequent production on renewed capital. The working class, by virtue of the surplus value produced in one year, creates that capital entering into relation with additional labour the next year. More capital is produced which, to have its value increased, comes into relation with more labour-power. Accumulation is ever-increasing. This increase points, for Marx, to the fact that some exchange must be of nonequivalents.

The laws of private property, according to Marx, "become by their own inner and inexorable dialectic changed into their very opposite;" the exchange of equivalents does not hold completely. When capital is exchanged (in the form of wages, means of subsistence) for labour-power, the unpaid labour of others is used for this purchase. The opposition or contradiction between the laws of exchange equivalence and the laws of capital accumulation is expressed quite succinctly by Marx: "The separation of property from labour has become the necessary consequence of a law that apparently originated in their identity" (n.d.: 547). The more exchange proliferates, the more property and labour separate, even though the classical development of value theory suggests that one's labour establishes one's property right in the product of that labour.

Four-fifths of the $10,000 ($8000) advanced in the above example may be invested in means of production (wool, wear and tear on the spinning machines) and one fifth ($2,000) may be paid in wages. If, furthermore, the workingday is half necessary labour-time (the period covering the $2,000 in wages) and half surplus labour-time, then $2,000 worth of surplus value in yarn also results. When this $2,000 is similarly advanced, an additional $400 worth of surplus results, and so on (See Marx n.d.: 543-44). Surplus value results from production and not circulation (of course the commodities produced must be sold, a fact which makes the capitalist's day much longer and more arduous than that of the aristocrat or feudal lord and which eventually results in the ruin of many would-be capitalists). Surplus value results from the products produced during surplus labour-time.

Labour *is* paid at its value, if by this we refer to its cost of production (how much abstract labour is embodied in the means of subsistence purchased by wages). It costs the capitalist class just this much to reproduce labour-power, the value-creating substance. In this sense it is an exchange of equivalents. If we refer, however, to the total value produced by labour in an entire working-day, then the surplus portion of this value is produced by unpaid labour; the exchange is of non-equivalents and capital accumulation is the result of unpaid labour.

The more capital is accumulated, the more additional labour-power must be employed on it. How much additional labour-power must be found for the profitable employment of capital? The ratio between constant capital (means) and variable capital (labour) is called "the organic composition of capital." This composition (the ratio) will change as more and more constant capital is accumulated. Marx takes this ratio as an average for all the industries in an entire society, and it expresses the comparative values of means of production and wages.

More and more value is incorporated in even more and more stuff. The value incorporated in material means grows more rapidly than the value of labour employed on it. As the productivity of labour increases, a given magnitude of value is incorporated in more things. The variable component becomes progressively smaller compared to the constant. A given amount of labour is embodied in a greater and greater quantity of things. The value of the mass of commodities rises, but not in proportion to their quantity. In the simplest terms, each item is worth less.

As capital accumulates, a lower and lower percentage of it is used to purchase labour-power. Proportionately, less and less labour-power is required for the productive employment of a given quantity of accumulated capital. The gain to be won per unit of production will decline. Since surplus value is created in production, the value of a commodity must be greater than its cost price. The rate of *profit*, therefore, is influenced primarily by this ratio and not simply by supply and demand. A commodity may be sold at a profit under its value:

> The excess value, or the surplus value, realised in the sale of a commodity appears to the capitalist as an excess of its selling price over its value, instead of an excess of its value over its cost-price, so that accordingly the surplus value incorporated in a

commodity is not realised through its sale, but springs
out of the sale itself. (1971: 38)

The cost price of a commodity (if the capitalist is to stay in
business) must be under its value and for surplus value to be
realized the capitalist must sell above cost-price. But the
amount of difference between value and cost price will vary
with the organic composition of capital. Given a constant
rate of surplus value, i.e., ratio of necessary to surplus labour
time, an increasing quantity of constant capital employed in
production relative to variable capital will necessarily entail
a falling rate of profit.

Using Marx's (1971: 211) examples, if the constant capital employed has a value of 50, half the working-day covers
wages and the other half creates surplus value, as stipulated
above, and the value of variable capital (that spent on wages)
is 100, then the rate of profit is 100/150 or 66²/₃%. On the
other hand, if the constant capital advanced is 300 and the
variable is still 100 (thus a shifting organic composition of
capital; less labour is required to process more means), the
rate of profit would be 100/400 or 25%.

> Since the mass of the employed living labour is
> continually on the decline as compared to the mass of
> materialized labour set in motion by it, i.e., to the
> productively consumed means of production, it follows
> that the portion of living labour, unpaid and congealed
> in surplus value, must also be continually on the
> decrease compared to the amount of value represented
> by the invested total capital. Since the ratio of the mass
> of surplus value to the value of the invested total capital
> forms the rate of profit, this rate must constantly fall.
> (1971: 213)

The total capital advanced rises more than the surplus value
produced and this, in turn, entails a falling rate of profit.

If it takes more and more material to embody a given
amount of surplus value, that value produced during surplus labour time, then the rate of profit per given mass of

product will fall. The total amount of profit, since so much more is produced, is still growing; yet, the falling *rate of profit* is nonetheless critical for the capitalist class and must be counteracted.

Recall the discussion of use-value and exchange-value above. An increase in use-values (more coats, for example) may at the same time be accompanied by a decrease in their exchange-value (as labour becomes more productive, a smaller portion of society's labour is congealed in each of them). This is the basic opposition or tension involved in the operation of capitalist relations. How can more value be produced and realized as surplus value as the rate of profit falls? How is this crisis to be met? The answer, in a few words, is growth, expansion. Anyone in business understands the significance of growth, and Marx is here attempting to un-cover the fundamental basis of this necessity. If profits are to be realized in such a way that they can continually renew the entire profit-making enterprise in spite of the fact that less and less value is incorporated in each individual item on the market, then, at least on the face of it, more and more must be produced cheaply enough to ensure market share and more must be sold. Streamlining the process, cheapen-ing labour, and finding more and more markets become the sine qua non of capitalism.

This is a critical situation which must be managed, and the means of this management is political. Colonial expan-sion, world wars, social welfare policies, and tariffs and taxes are all expressions of the efforts of the state in different soci-eties to manage this crisis. On occasion, these are also ex-pressions of competition between groups of capitalists, but on the whole, they reflect the basic requirement of capital accumulation to reproduce wage labour. A substantial por-tion of the world's population must be kept in a position of needing to sell their labour-power to survive and thus play their role in the production of value which is alienated as the property of others.

Alienation is a concept which Marx developed from the work of Hegel and his Young Hegelian followers. For these predecessors, alienation was a result of the labour of consciousness and reflected a loss of true understanding. For Marx, however, alienation is the result of physical labour under the conditions of a capitalist society, the loss of one's product and with that the loss of control over life-activity more generally. The usage of this term in Marx's later work is designed to emphasize the class nature of capitalist production. Property is here private property, and the work of wage labourers serves to produce this property for others. Capital and labour are separated under these conditions, and the political economy of Marx's day assumed this separation but provided no explanation of its emergence. The work of wage labourers produces a force hostile toward themselves.

It is in *The Economic and Philosophic Manuscripts of 1844* that Marx outlined his notion of alienation and, although this is early in his career, this outline still reflects his shift to a critique of political economy. "The direct relationship of labour to its produce is the relationship of the worker to the objects of his production" (Marx 1978: 73). In a society where the separation of capital, labour, and landed property obtains, the worker is the slave of the object s/he produces. As labourers who sell their labour-power, they produce objects, objectifications of their activity, which confront them as something alien, as another's property. These processes of objectification, estrangement, and alienation are the results of their activity under these conditions.

The more they produce, the more do they enrich and empower the forces against them, and the more do they rob their environment of materials for the satisfaction of their own needs, needs for their own projects and their own physical existence. As workers, they are merely physical subjects, and as physical subjects they exist only as workers; they are reduced to means of production.

The worker is estranged from practical life-activity in three senses:

1. s/he is estranged from the products of his/her labour;
2. s/he is estranged from the activity of labour;
3. workers are estranged from each other.

Firstly, the product of labour is an objectification; labour is realized in an object. This object is lost to the worker and is appropriated by someone else. Political economy describes the loss and appropriation but makes it appear natural. In fact, the more objects the worker produces, the fewer can s/he possess; in becoming the owners' property, the objects empower owners against workers. One's labour not only becomes an object but becomes an object hostile and alien to the worker.

Secondly, the worker is estranged from his/her activity, from him/herself. As did the object of labour, so does the activity of labour become the property of someone else. Labour-power is purchased. This is a "labour of self-sacrifice, of mortification" (Marx 1978: 74). This labour is not engaged to satisfy a need of the labourer but rather the need of someone external to the producer. Productive activity is thus not one's own activity. This is "self-estrangement."

Finally, the life of the species, collective life, is turned into a means of individual life only. Workers are thus estranged from each other. The life one may lead collectively is turned into a means to satisfy the individual life of someone else. People's lives can become an object for them only when they lead a collective life. In this case, however, this social, collective resource is turned into a mere means of staying alive.

As the forces arrayed against the labourers become more powerful and, at the same time, the falling rate of profit makes the situation more and more critical for the capitalist class, measures are taken to continue to reproduce the capital/wage labour relation necessary to the accumulation process.

Accumulation is accompanied by increase in the productivity of labour. Since more and more surplus product is converted into means of production, more labour is initially needed in the branches of industry where this is occurring. This must be supplied without taking too many workers away from other branches, even though the increased productivity tends to decrease the demand for labour. An "industrial reserve army" is kept unemployed or underemployed in order to keep a supply of inexpensive labour ready at hand for expansion. The price of labour is kept low by deskilling and hiring those who may be assumed under certain conditions to have lower expectations, such as women, immigrants, or children. Exploitation is increased by lengthening the working-day and making labour more intense, depressing wages by cheapening the means of subsistence, maintaining the industrial reserve army, and by engaging in foreign trade to acquire cheaper raw materials and means of subsistence (See Marx 1971: 232-40).

Thus, Marx's concepts of capital, crisis, and contradiction all turn on the fundamental class character of society and on modern capitalist society's specific configuration of classes. His notion of the state reflects this basis. In fact, it is more difficult to generalize about the state than about other entities and relations because its particular character will change according to the specific relations and conditions found in each society. The works of Marx in which this notion is most thoroughly discussed are highly detailed, historical-political studies of specific events in particular countries.

We have examined the nature of capital, its crises, and the dependence of capital on the class relations of capitalist society. For capital to function, there must be maintained a class of persons needing to sell their labour-power to survive, and as crises are encountered, steps are taken to ensure its cheap supply. The profits of merchants, the rent of landowners, and the interest of financiers must be reckoned into the equation which allows for ever-increasing value. These relations are quite complex, and their stable regulation is a highly nuanced affair.

How is all of this regulated and controlled? The simple answer to this question is: In the interest of the dominant class. There are, however, a number of considerations which make this question and answer much too simple and ultimately insufficient in detail. Firstly, what do we mean by interest and in exactly whose interest is this regulation carried out? Secondly, what is the precise nature of this regulating agency and of its relation to the various interests found in society?

First of all, this agency is called the state and, at the highest level of abstraction, it can be seen to control in the interest of the dominant class, now the capitalist class. So the actions of the state are conducted on the basis of class interest. Taxes are levied, trade regulations enacted, and social welfare expanded or cut back, all in the interest of capital or of its representatives.

It is tempting, at this point, to imagine that capitalists regulate in their own interests. According to this formulation, however, the state *is* the capitalist class. But these are not wholly congruent. There would be no need of a concept of the state if this were the case. Remember that Marx has already maintained that once society is divided, the state emerges; no division of labour or classes — no state. The state grows out of — is an excrescence of — society. In fact, we have a state when we have society rather than a virtually undivided community. The essence, as it were, of the state is the particular divided and oppositional character of society, and the essence of the modern state is the oppositional character of civil society.

The notion of civil society is prominent in the work of Hegel, and Marx laboured to correct what he saw as Hegel's identification of the state with what was reasonable in historical development. The development of the state, for Hegel, represented what was morally and socially purer than or superior to the development of civil society and, in fact, the Prussian state of his day represented, in his view, a model for human relations and their governance. Marx, on the other hand, saw the state as growing out of precisely those class oppositions which would have to be overcome, if, indeed, any progress toward understandable and intelligible relations with others and toward nature were to be achieved.

According to Hegel, the state represents and embodies a general or public interest and, for this reason, is the best model for society to attempt to follow. Marx, rather, tended to view such general interest as a fiction and saw the state instead as derivative from the class nature of society. He proceeded to detail the specific interests involved in particular historical developments and struggles. These detailed analyses display the impossibility of viewing the state as upholding the specific interests of any particular members or factions. Capitalists, for example, are competing not only with wage labourers but also with each other. They compete within a given industry as well as between industries and between nations. Policies favouring financiers will not necessarily favour industrialists at the same time. Politics, like housework, is never done. There are many conflicting interests; no one of them is utterly powerful. Yet, the state rules in the interest of the capitalist class.

No one willed the socio-economic relations in which we find ourselves. They were not designed by anyone but are addressed by interested parties by means of varied access to state, law, military, and police. They tend to be maintained in the face of other forces tending to tear them asunder. This "economic base," for Marx as opposed to Hegel, gives shape to the character of the state and law, "the superstructure." This becomes most clearly evident during times of political upheaval, and Marx's detailed analyses focus on such periods. It is in *The 18th Brumaire of Louis Bonaparte*, concerning the development and action of the state in the upheavals of mid-nineteenth century France, that Marx's writing is at its most detailed and incisive: Napoleon III could not, despite what he claimed, give to one class without taking from another. The English enthusiasm about the beauties of the English monarchy and constitution proves that in reality the English authorities of the day were "enthusiastic only about ground rent" (Marx 47-8; 13233); they were supportive of a particular set of relations favouring landlords.

According to Marx, societies have been marked by the exploitation of one class by another ever since they began to display divisions. For him, this is neither natural nor inevitable. In all his work, Marx emphasized the movement and development of different kinds of social relations. In each form of class-divided society, there exists a tension between the exploiter class and the exploited class. It is this kind of tension which is responsible for the movement or development of history. While part of Marx's theory is devoted to understanding the condition of each stage of history, i.e., how each form of class-divided society reproduces itself, he also theorized about the crises and transitions produced by this tension. Slaves, serfs, and wage labourers have all, at various times, revolted. In the case of the first two, their masters ultimately proved incapable of containing the movement or transition to another form of society.

In the case of the first two transitions, from antiquity to feudalism and from feudalism to capitalism, a group existing within the interstices of the previous society took over as the dominant or ruling class and turned out to be the new exploiters. Marx was concerned to theorize about the possibility of these tensions and transitions facilitating a movement toward an ultimately non-exploitative status. His hope for this rested with the proletariat, the class of wage labourers exploited by the bourgeoisie in a capitalist society. He hoped his close examination of capitalist society would reveal, first of all, some of the fundamental oppositions and contradictions in that society and, secondly, some of the tendencies and possibilities contained in those tensions.

In his view, the proletariat was the first class in history not simply to attempt to free itself from bondage, but by attempting to free itself, to end exploitation of any kind. Already in discussing Hegel's *Philosophy of Right*, Marx indicated his suspicion that it was the proletariat that would be the historical agent to change conditions. Religion, he argued, represented the "flower" which disguised the real chains holding people in bondage. The criticism of the Young Hegelians had removed the flower to expose the chains. The point was to break the chains. This accomplishment required a class with "radical chains." The proletariat, Marx argued, was bound in such a profound way that it could not free itself without ending exploitation altogether.

His notion of this historical agency changed and developed as he continued to analyze capitalist society. In *The Communist Manifesto*, he and Engels outlined what was to become the most famous of his assertions concerning this revolutionary task. This work begins with the assertion that, "[t]he history of all hitherto existing society is the history of class struggle" (Marx and Engels 1978: 472). In the case of the capitalist society of his day, Marx made note of the practice and necessity of the globalization of capitalist relations. The forms of competition already mentioned in *Wage Labour and Capital* made such tremendous expansion necessary. Expanding markets, the constant need to keep pools of cheap labour ready at hand, and continuous increases in the productivity of labour (revolutionizing the instruments of labour) to ensure market share, all work to ensure a very direct and brutal form of exploitation. At the same time, all of this creates the tendency to divide society into two great classes, the bourgeoisie and proletariat. Capital, property, and political power become more and more centralized, and more and more people sink to the level of the proletariat, unable to compete with larger capitalists. These globalizing, centralizing, and concentrating tendencies produce, at the same time, the possibility of an international association of the proletariat. Modern industry tends of itself to organize the workers.

For Marx and Engels the main upshot of all this is that with the vast increases in productivity produced by capitalism there comes a brutalization of the lives of the producers of that wealth. They are also, by virtue of the way in which capitalist production organizes them, in a position to fight to end such exploitation. The relations of production, class exploitation in its capitalist form, at a certain point prevents any further apparently equitable expansion of this productivity.

> The essential condition for the existence, and for the sway of the bourgeois class, is the formation and augmentation of capital; the condition for capital is wage labour. Wage labour rests exclusively on competition between the labourers. The advance of industry, whose involuntary promoter is the bourgeoisie, replaces the isolation of the labourers, due to competition, by their revolutionary combination, due to association. The development of Modern Industry, therefore, cuts from under its feet the very foundation on which the bourgeoisie produces and appropriates

products. What the bourgeoisie, therefore, produces, above all, is its own grave-diggers. Its fall and the victory of the proletariat are equally inevitable. (Marx and Engels 1978: 483)

Thus, according to Marx and Engels, given all these tendencies, the bourgeoisie will eventually prove unable to maintain the relations of capitalist society. The rebellions of 1848 failed, however, and Marx continued to analyze more thoroughly the conditions and relations he thought might eventually lead to the overcoming of these relations of production.

There is a tendency toward crisis which will ultimately prove unmanageable for the capitalists. Today we can witness the movement of enterprises to countries with cheaper labour and the push also to expand markets to more countries. Capitalists are fast running out of places to do this. For Marx, this meant the opportunity for revolutionary action on the part of the proletariat. This, of course, has not happened. In recent years, the significance of the proletariat in visions of social transformation has tended to be downplayed.

3

Emile Durkheim
(1858-1917)

Emile Durkheim probably did more than anyone else to establish sociology as an academic discipline. Like Comte and other early sociologists, he was concerned about social integration and stability. Sociology represented, for Durkheim, an effort to discover the necessary ingredients for national unity and stability, but, unlike Comte, his plans for intervention were less aggressive and his thought less hypothetical. Whereas Comte's concern with order may be seen as a response to the uncertain and ambiguous results of the French Revolution, Durkheim's parallel interests may be seen as a result of the event which ended that ambiguity, France's defeat in the Franco-Prussian War in 1870. The intervening century had been politically uncertain, but after the defeat those who favoured a rational, industrial society (to compete with Germany) began to carry the day.

The weakness highlighted by the defeat itself was amplified for Durkheim by the fact that anti-semitic sentiment was aroused to provide a scapegoat for the French defeat. Durkheim was himself a Jew from the town of Espinal near Strasbourg, and his father was a prominent rabbi in the region. In fact, Durkheim had himself been a rabbinical student but later became an atheist, perhaps in keeping with the rational, secular approach to social integration which he came to view as the only way to produce a strong, cohesive France. A couple of decades later, he became involved in a very famous case of anti-semitism in which a Jewish army officer, Colonel Dreyfus, was falsely accused of espionage on behalf of the Germans.

He visited Germany in 1885-86 in order to learn what he could about the state of social science in that country, and it irritated him that sociology, born in France, had developed more fully in Germany. His first publications were reviews of German works. In these assessments he found the systematic, empirical, collective focus to his liking, but he went on to prefer his own distinct version of social realism. *L'Année Sociologique*, the journal founded by Durkheim in 1898, did much to raise the quality and status of French sociology. In the midst of the next war with Germany, in which he lost his son, he died in 1917.

Among the intellectual influences on Durkheim were several followers of Comte at the Ecole Normale Superieure. Studying with his teacher Emile Boutroux, he came to view sociology as having a distinct method and field. Perhaps of even more influence was the philosopher Charles Renouvier, whose brand of rationalism recommended a scientific approach to social cohesion and morality while upholding the notion of the autonomy of the individual. For Renouvier, the Kantian doctrine of the categories (discussed above in the introduction to Marx) did produce viable objects of knowledge. Unlike Kant, however, Durkheim thought that these categories, such as space, time, and causality, changed their specific character, and thus were not universal features of the human mind but had different meanings in different times and places. This notion developed into Durkheim's claim that categories of thought are socially determined since they are different in different societies. He also had two scientifically and sociologically oriented history instructors at the Ecole, Gabriel Monod and Fustel de Coulanges. His contact with their brand of sociological history provided a factual basis for the kind of generalizations emanating from Comte and Spencer. His first university appointment in education was at Bordeaux, where he replaced Alfred Espinas who had combined Spencer's notion of organic evolution with Comte's idea of society as based on ideas.

For the most part, he stayed away from day-to-day politics in favour of his academic projects, although he did discuss St. Simon and other socialist ideas with his friend Jean

Jaures at the Ecole. In fact, he authored a separate work (1958) on the ideas of the man thought to be the founder of modern socialist ideas, Henri St. Simon. Not only does his treatment of St. Simon reflect a less than hostile attitude toward socialism, but Durkheim credits him with being a more consistent formulator of positivism than Comte. The former had emphasized not only the growth of mind as progenitor of science but also the growth of forms of social organization. Socialism, in Durkheim's view, contrary to both communism and modern liberal economics, tended to focus on questions of proper regulation and integration.

Given the increasingly secular nature of European societies as well as their advanced complexity, he searched for a scientific, rational way to provide for the integration and stability so desired but whose foundation in non-rational, religious traditions was evaporating. One had to know the features of a well integrated society (which elements were essential and how they were related) in order to make any suggestions for its establishment. Above all, he wanted to secure sociology as the discipline which would be recognized as capable of providing the intellectual tools necessary for this project.

To accomplish this, Durkheim proposed to distinguish sociology in terms of the subject matter to which it was suitably applied and in terms of a special realm of facts over which it alone had jurisdiction. Other disciplines had, in his view, failed to accomplish a rational, empirical, and systematic study of the harmonizing factors of collective life. There are thus features of collective existence, he argued, which are not reducible to features of the atoms, individuals, which make it up. These features are not studied by any other discipline. Philosophy, biology, and psychology studied various elements of the important issues, but none of them systematically studied the essential characteristics of collective life.

Thus, there are features of this group existence which can and should govern individual behaviour, at least for the most part. These features are products of collective, group life and do not emanate from the individual. On occasion, they are in need of repair, but the daily practices, beliefs, and

consciousness of a people cannot be reduced to nor originally located in individuals. Collective, social, moral forces
in the form of shared beliefs (representations, knowledge,
images, symbols), on the one hand, and in the form of organizational structures and divisions, on the other, tend, in
his view, to govern and integrate the practices and behaviours of individual members. Both organizational and symbolic features of social life were important in Durkheim's
analysis of unity and solidarity.

Perhaps his own life is representative of the trend toward
secularization which was evident in his society. Rational,
scientific investigation characterized modern thought, and
society, in his view, now needed and could make use of rational, scientific bases for integration. Members were now
in such a condition that they could rationally understand
the basis for their unity in society and no longer needed reli-
giously-based forms of solidarity. Sociology, therefore, was
to provide this rational understanding.

Durkheim's formal education was primarily in philosophy, history, and education. His thesis was in philosophy,
and he later revised and published this as *The Division of
Labour in Society*. Here, we already see his abiding concern
with unity and solidarity, and he defends modern society as
capable, in principle, of rational integration while fostering
individual autonomy. While at Bordeaux, he completed the
revisions to *The Division of Labour* as well as publishing
The Rules of Sociological Method and *Suicide*. *Rules* represents the formal presentation of frameworks and procedures
already initiated in *The Division of Labour*. In the work, he
outlines his concept of *social facts*, that realm of facts underlying phenomena which are irreducibly social. These are ways
of thinking, acting, and feeling whose origin in collective life
is outside the individual. *Suicide* represents his attempt to
demonstrate that suicide, an individual, anti-social act, can
be understood sociologically. Whatever the "reasons" individuals may have for this act, sociology alone is capable of
understanding the factors contributing to varying *rates* of
such acts, factors having to do with faulty regulation of individual tendencies.

Durkheim achieved a position at the Sorbonne in Paris and continued his work, primarily in religion and education. In *Primitive Classification*, written with his nephew, Marcel Mauss, he sets out to demonstrate the social, organizational basis of logic and forms of thought. Conceptions of nature, the classification of things in the world, are shown to parallel the organization or classification of groups and individuals in society. Social authority is seen as the unconscious basis for this kind of phenomenon. This phenomenon, furthermore, is also seen as the basis for further developments and refinements in traditions of human thought. Advanced understandings of nature, such as had developed since the advent of modern science, were seen to rest on such a basis. The advance of the division of labour, in Durkheim's view, was responsible for the rationalization of forms of knowledge. This is part and parcel of the argument in the last work published during his lifetime, *The Elementary Forms of The Religious Life*. In this work, he argues that the basis of religiously conceived moral authority and suasion lie, in fact, in an impersonal, anonymous, collective, social, and moral authority. Whereas the believer sees this force as divine in origin, Durkheim argues that it represents the complex assertion of collective, group forces. He goes on in this work to suggest that the *development* of conceptions of nature and society, beginning on this basis, concludes with specialized forms of thought and investigation (science) which parallel the nature of the phenomena they describe more and more closely. Thought and collective life reflect the nature of things ever more closely as they develop through the specialization inherent in human history. Such specialized, rational, and empirically-based knowledge is also seen to provide the basis for solidarity in modern society.

Thought, according to Durkheim, precedes conduct. The basis of thought was a contested issue in his day, and Durkheim joined the fray in an effort to establish the relative autonomy and significance of what he termed "collective representations." He took issue first and foremost with those who purported that neural physiology could account for conduct and for perception. Against them, he argued that even though it makes sense to claim that experience is the result of the sensory excitation of neural pathways, this cannot account for the various memories of perceptions and certainly not for the thoughtful comparisons of ideas, images, conceptions, and arguments in terms of their points of similarity and difference. Such processes of thought and conduct, argued Durkheim, although dependent for their functioning on healthy neural pathways, are processes that work with memories and conceptions; in short, they are representations which enjoy what he called a relative autonomy from their neural basis. In other words, the logic by which ideas and conceptions are grouped or analyzed is not itself to be found in systems of neurons. They may owe much to neural function for their production but, once produced, they are relatively independent and obey laws of their own.

Representations are indeed caused, but they are themselves the causes of conduct (Durkheim 1974: 4). Similar representations may entail a similar state of the nerve cells, but the representations themselves comprise a distinct and relatively independent order of facts. Thus Durkheim asserts the existence of something like mind as related to but distinguishable from brain. One idea, for example, may evoke another; it can "put us in mind of" the other. The grounds upon which these ideas may be similar or related is not based on physiology. The parts of ideas are related by their own laws of combination which are not strictly parallel to the parts of neural processes. This is a relationship *sui generis*, of its own kind. Durkheim is not interested in making metaphysical or ontological arguments about the precise status of representations. It is sufficient for him that they are relatively autonomous from biology, and that their effects can be observed. We are not necessarily conscious of this process even as we participate in it, just as we are not conscious of neural synapses in processes of sensation.

Just as individual representations are relatively independent of their neural basis, so are collective representations relatively independent of the individual representations whose processes of collective association produce them. Thus, for Durkheim, there exists a realm of relatively autonomous collective representations resulting from the group life of individuals and which, in turn, effect the conduct of those individuals.

> While one might perhaps contest the statement that all social facts without exception impose themselves from without upon the individual, the doubt does not seem possible as regards religious beliefs and practices, the rules of morality and the innumerable precepts of law that is to say, all the most characteristic manifestations of collective life. All are expressly obligatory, and this obligation is the proof that these ways of acting and thinking are not the work of the individual but come from a moral power above him, that which the mystic calls God or which can be more scientifically conceived. (Durkheim 1974: 25)

Although we may disagree with religious doctrine, especially with its religious, supernatural features, Durkheim's point is that, nonetheless, it exists and exerts a force in daily life. These are collective phenomena and as such comprise a distinct order of facts which must be understood or explained by means of the properties of the whole, by means of collective representations.

Durkheim distinguishes physiological reality from what he calls spiritual reality — the mental life of the individual. (Bear in mind that by the term "spiritual" he means to indicate the significance of mental phenomena and not something supernatural.) Similarly, he distinguishes this spiritual reality from what he calls the "hyperspiritual" — a collective mental reality. It helps to think of this as cultural reality as opposed to the individual mental life. Each individual has his/her own experiential angle or slant, but collective representations are available to all members.

Collective representations comprise, according to Durkheim, a realm of moral facts. These representations have not only authoritative power in the form of obligations, but they are also desirable. "It is this *sui generis* desirability which is commonly called good" (Durkheim 1974: 36). Moral phenomena, in Durkheim's view, have this dual character of obligation and desirability much as the sacred character of religious doctrine and deity is not only feared but loved. He is at pains, first of all, to present a clear understanding of the features of collective moral life and, secondly, to propose remedies for crises in contemporary moral regulation. Such was the aim of his first major work, *The Division of Labour.*

CONSCIOUSNESS, LAW AND THE HISTORY OF SOLIDARITY

As MENTIONED, Durkheim's *Division of Labour in Society* is in part an attempt to discover the grounds of solidarity and unity in modern, industrial society. He wanted to carry out a systematic, scientific investigation of solidarity with a view to establishing its essential elements and thus also establish sociology as the discipline needed for its restoration. Modern society had its detractors in Durkheim's day, those who saw the rise in anti-social phenomena such as crime and suicide as produced by the increasingly complex division of labour. Although the increased division of labour was accompanied by an increase in these phenomena, Durkheim argued that it was not responsible for them. The argument in his first major work is an attempt to demonstrate that the division of labour provides a firm basis for solidarity.

In setting out to demonstrate that the division of labour is a moral phenomenon, Durkheim was at pains to illustrate that it concerns the bonds or connections between people in society. He thus needed some evidence, some kind of concrete indicator, of these moral connections. If he could find such an indicator, he thought, he would have evidence that the division of labour was, indeed, a moral phenomenon. This observable indicator was law, written or otherwise. Law governs connections between people, is identifiable, and so provides evidence of the kind of connections existing in a given society.

It is an observable expression of the sort of moral bonds existing in a society at a given time. He thus set out to study legal/moral development systematically with a view to tracing the different factors affecting forms of bonds, of unity and solidarity. He decided that there were two fundamental bases for solidarity, likeness and interdependence.

Durkheim hoped to uncover the "facts of the moral life" by scientific means. These facts, he argues, endure the test of time if they are of use to society, and he recommends intervention when these laws break down. The division of labour, he tried to demonstrate, helps to fulfil contradictory needs, individual uniqueness and solidarity. Although there are abnormal states in its development, the division of labour is, in the end, the basis for a firm and lasting form of solidarity. The demand imposed on the individual by the division of labour to "make yourself usefully fulfil a determinate function" (1964: 43), is not fundamentally in opposition to any requirement of social solidarity. This socially and morally based demand, Durkheim argues, is the legal basis for the strongest form of solidarity. We can specialize and all fulfil a common ideal in doing so.

First, we must rid ourselves of traditional, unscientific notions of the moral life. This "methodical doubt" is necessary to ferret out the true causes and functions of the division of labour and to present the abnormal cases, those requiring intervention. The relevant order of facts is to be subjected to scientific scrutiny; we must discover an objective element in them, even a measurable one (1964: 37). He begins with the question of the needs of the social organism. We must find the need supplied by the division of labour and then determine whether this need is a moral one. The division of labour fulfils a moral need if it is to underlie order, harmony and social solidarity.

Finding the objective or possibly measurable element in the right order of facts requires us to discover an external index of internal facts. This is the law; it is an index of states of consciousness. The more relations in a society, the more solid it is; since laws govern relations, the more laws there are, the more relations there are. These laws are of two basic kinds since solidarity has two basic roots, likeness and difference. We shall consider the case of likeness first.

In the case of a society with minimal internal differentiation, likeness is therefore the basis of solidarity. In such a society, people are not divided very much as to function. They live remarkably similar lives, tend to know one another in fairly small communities, and share many ideas, beliefs, and experiences. The law which governs relations in such a society tends to be what Durkheim calls *repressive law*. There is a high degree of consensus, since so much is shared, about the highly significant do's and don'ts of the society. Actions which transgress these prescriptions are, for Durkheim, crimes. To find out what a crime is, says Durkheim, we look not for specific kinds of actions, not those which might be considered heinous, nor those which might be thought to be damaging to society, but rather those which provoke the reaction called *punishment*. To know what a crime is in any society, we look to see what gets punished. Punishment, in a simple society tends to be expiative; suffering on the part of the transgressor is demanded.

Transgression are against what Durkheim calls the *common conscience*. (The French "conscience" connotes both the English "conscience" and "consciousness"; the French implies both moral and cognitive functions. The terms for this entity are either common conscience or collective consciousness.) This term is defined as the totality of shared beliefs which comprise the strong do's and don'ts of the society. They are strongly held, firmly engraven, and highly specific beliefs, the transgression of which constitutes a crime. Transgression, furthermore, is met by the characteristic response called punishment, in this case expiative punishment. Thus, if someone transgresses against one of these strongly held beliefs, it constitutes an offense against the common conscience, not against some calculated notion of harm to society or well-being. A crime, for Durkheim, is whatever offends the common conscience.

Thus, in a society with a relatively undeveloped division of labour, one in which people do not fulfil a large variety of specialized functions, law tends to be repressive. This law is usually unwritten, and a violation of one of its elements is a shock to an underlying sentiment which is given observable expression in the law. These sentiments expressed in law must not only be firmly held and strongly engraven in the consciousness of members but also must be highly specific. A wayward son, for example, is not a criminal. No expiative punishment is prescribed for this ill-defined drifting. But a statement such as "Do not eat the flesh of the animal for which your clan is named" indicates that severe punishment awaits the potential transgressor.

For Durkheim, "[a]n act is criminal when it offends strong and defined states of the collective conscience" (1964: 80). An act is defined as criminal because it shocks the common conscience, not the other way around. Crime enfeebles the common conscience; our reaction is a struggle against this enfeeblement, hence, the punishment response. The reaction has nothing to do with deterrence or providing examples to potential wrongdoers. The reaction springs from a "temper" which is everyone's without being anyone's in particular. The fact that there is crime at all, however, indicates that the sentiments involved are not representations for absolutely everyone.

The definition of and resistance to crime is a thoroughly collective matter for Durkheim. Individuals, upon witnessing a forbidden act, for example, do not ponder consequences and weigh heavily the pros and cons before responding with an act of punishment. Rather, it is the common conscience which itself responds through them. Crime, in fact, unifies the "like-minded." For Durkheim, punishment is accounted for by collective sentiments. Essential likenesses are expressed in this way. Durkheim thus posits the existence of two distinct but related consciousnesses, individual and collective. We know and comprehend others by virtue of the common conscience; states which are personal to us form our individual consciousness. This position constitutes one of the best known features of Durkheim's thought, the assumption of a *homo duplex*, a "dual" human nature.

The type of solidarity manifest in the type of society described above is called "mechanical." Because the differences between component parts of this kind of society are slight, the connections are between similar persons or groups. The parts do not exhibit significant differences from one another, nor do the parts of a machine, hence, *mechanical solidarity*. Connections are between segments, similarly constituted parts made of essentially the same material. If a segment or individual is deleted, no integral, special function necessary to the whole is lost.

As Durkheim traced the development of law, he found a major transition from repressive to *restitutive law*. This difference indicates a difference in type of solidarity. Restitutive law carries no expiative sanction. Suffering is not demanded; the transgressor is compelled to return things to the initial state of affairs, that which obtained before the alleged wrongdoing. This kind of law exists outside the common conscience. Nonetheless, it is related to solidarity, argues Durkheim. This transition in law is traced from ancient Hebrew through Roman and Salic to modern French law. In the case of each transition there remains an element of criminal or repressive law, but by the time we arrive at the modern French case, by far the largest portion of the law is no longer penal or repressive in character. It is, rather, contractual or restitutive.

Under such moral/legal conditions, a transgression requires that a given state of affairs be returned, by actions of the transgressor, to an original state. S/he makes restitution. In simple terms, if I break your window, I replace it or give you the money value of the replacement; society does not require cutting off the hand which threw the errant rock or ball. This difference in moral/legal conditions, according to Durkheim, is made possible by a more advanced division of labour. Wherever there is a more complex division of labour we tend to share less (we have, after all, less in the way of similar experience and so share less in the way of beliefs and consciousness); our relations and connections are governed less by the common conscience. Relations between us under these newer conditions tend to be more contractually negotiated. Contractual negotiations are, furthermore, regulated by a different kind of law. Contract law generally stipulates that one should live up to contracts. If a contract, whether business or marriage for example, is breached, the transgressor must make restitution. If any undue advantage is achieved or damage is done to another party, the original undamaged condition must be restored by the transgressor. If I agree to pay you $500 in instalments but stop making payments after paying $100, you can take me to small claims court to recover the $400 (plus costs). I am unlikely to be banished from society or to be drawn and quartered.

In the kind of society characterized by a more advanced division of labour, we are interdependent. We do not, as in the more simple society, perform similar activities and thus completely share experience, beliefs, and consciousness. We do, however, perform different and essential tasks for the maintenance of each other and of the whole. This material and organizational difference provides for a different kind of law and a different kind of solidarity. This newer kind of solidarity is called *organic solidarity*. As organs are to the body, so are branches of the division of labour and other institutions to the social whole. These are not similarly constituted segments mechanically attached to one another. Each is qualitatively different from the other and performs a different function in the maintenance of the whole. Just as the heart, liver, and brain, for example, provide various, different functions for the life of the body, so, too, do various institutions and branches of the division of labour perform different functions for the life of society.

Under such conditions, Durkheim argues, individual uniqueness and specialization exist alongside a common ideal in the maintenance of organic solidarity. The negotiating parties to contracts are not absolutely free to set any and all terms they want when striking these contracts. This is why, for Durkheim, there exists contract *law*. There are many conditions and stipulations governing contracts. Society, even when characterized by organic solidarity and an advanced division of labour, appears as a "third party" to all contracts. Social, moral authority still lurks behind this brand of solidarity in the form of restitutive law.

The autonomous, independent individual is thus, as Goldmann has suggested (see Chapter 1), a product of history, rather than its point of departure. Most importantly, in Durkheim's terms, if we are to be significantly different one from another, the opportunity for us to be different kinds of people must exist. For Durkheim, this permits us to "have our cake and eat it too," to be unique individuals and to live in a unified society with common ideals and aims. These are not, in his view, fundamentally contradictory goals.

Mechanical solidarity is produced by a strong common conscience which, in turn, depends on the undifferentiated segments of a society in which there is not much specialization of function. The elements of the common conscience are firmly held, strongly engraven and highly specific beliefs, the transgression of which elicits the response of expiative punishment (hence, repressive law). This response to crime is produced in and through us by the common conscience. Therefore, crime actually serves the function of uniting us and strengthening the common conscience.

As functions become more specialized, and people become significantly different from one another in some ways, the significance of the common conscience dwindles. Their dependence on one another increases, however, due to this very specialization, and, as a result, people enjoy connections regulated primarily by restitutive rather than repressive sanctions. In this organic solidarity, social authority still regulates connections by means of restitutive law.

Mechanical solidarity is based on an "organized totality of beliefs and sentiments common to all members of the group," while organic solidarity is based on definite relations uniting different, special functions. We do not find pure instances of either type. Different societies, however, will exhibit a preponderance of one or the other. Distinctive personalities are less evident in the first type and really become a possibility only in the second. Durkheim outlines the following analogies to illustrate the two types of solidarity:

> The social molecules which can be coherent in this way can act together only in the measure that they have no actions of their own, as the molecules of inorganic bodies. That is why we propose to call this type of solidarity mechanical. (Durkheim 1964: 130)

The more labour is divided, the more dependent each of us is on society; the more specialized we are the more personal is our activity.

> This solidarity resembles that which we observe among the higher animals. Each organ, in effect, has its special physiognomy, its autonomy. And, moreover, the unity of the organism is as great as the individuation of the parts is more marked. Because of this analogy, we propose to call the solidarity which is due to the division of labour, organic. (Durkheim 1964: 131)

The indicator of the type of solidarity manifested in a given society is the type of law. "(I)n order to recognize their respective importance in a given social type, it is enough to compare the respective extent of the two types of law which express them, since law always varies as the social relations which it governs" (Durkheim 1964: 132). Over the course of the history of societies, in particular the history of the development of the division of labour, we witness the emergence of more restitutive law and the recession of penal law.

We are now bound to society by ties having less to do with common beliefs and more with united, specialized functions. In earlier forms of society, argues Durkheim, whole groups could secede without changing the nature of the whole; this kind of society is therefore less solid. Mechanical solidarity links people less strongly and, over the course of history, grows weaker. Segmental organization with a clan base will yield a repressive law with a basis in the common conscience. Specialized organization with an occupational base will yield restitutive law with a basis in the division of labour.

Thus, occupational organizations are, for Durkheim, the key to solidarity in modern societies. Only abnormal causes, he states (1964: 190), prevent the division of labour from providing the required level of solidarity. In the first place, the division of labour develops and becomes more complex because of increases in what Durkheim calls *moral volume* and *moral density*. Moral volume refers to the overall number of individuals, and moral density refers to the number of relations between persons in a given kind of society. Individuals act and react on one another in more and different ways. When there are more relations between individuals, there is higher moral density. When both moral volume and density grow, we have more relations between more persons. It is this condition, for Durkheim, which produces the development of the division of labour, of specialization and, hence, of restitutive law.

The earlier form of segmented society must undergo certain changes before the division of labour can appear. The segments must begin to disappear or join together. The drive toward cooperation and specialization then comes from increases in volume and density. The more this material and organizational milieu stimulates our intellect and sensibilities, the more civilization and the division of labour develop. There are, however, abnormal forms of the division of labour in which organic solidarity is not all that it should be. "If the division of labour does not produce solidarity in all these cases, it is because the relations of the organs are not regulated, because they are in a state of *anomy*" (Durkheim 1964: 388).

Following Comte, Durkheim held that the state arises as a special organ for unifying a diverse society. The state, furthermore, needs special advice in order to perform this regulating and integrating function and in order to limit conflict. It must ensure that all the conditions for the promotion of organic solidarity are present.

The rapidity of the growth of the division of labour, of markets, and other elements of modern society has produced a condition of anomie, of normlessness. New norms which might ordinarily regulate conduct within and between spheres have not had time to form, and the old norms have ceased to be relevant under the new conditions.

The necessary regulation can be provided with the help of sociology. Such help, for Durkheim, is a response to a crisis in professional ethics. The norms of conduct within and between branches of the division of labour, occupations, and professions can be provided by an intermediate corporate group, roughly based on the medieval guild. Once this is accomplished, routines of regular contact between persons would be established, and those persons would not be without common aims and determinate functions. Norms are important because they place limits on individual needs and desires and, thus, make possible the actual satisfaction of such needs and desires. Where norms are clear and strong, anomie is greatly reduced. People are thus linked together in a lasting way through a system of rights and duties, the need for which is understood and embraced by all.

Durkheim thus set himself two basic tasks in the conclusion to the *Division of Labour in Society*: to illustrate the opportunities for individual expression and difference provided by the division of labour simultaneously with the provision of a strong, unifying force; and to find explanations other than the growth and complexity of the division of labour for conflict and crisis. In cases where the unifying force is lacking, sociology is employed to determine how it might be restored.

Like other social facts and phenomena, the division of labour displays pathological forms and it is these, rather than the division of labour per se, which are responsible for anti-social phenomena and disunity. In his day, Durkheim witnessed what he called "commercial and industrial crises" marked by business failures and a highly developed conflict between capital and labour. To him, these represent "partial breaks in organic solidarity" (Durkheim 1964: 354).

Extensive specialization can destroy unity, especially in a large enterprise. Individual functionaries may feel that rewards for their efforts are small, and that there is little opportunity to comprehend and identify with the purpose of the whole and their role within it. Under such conditions, experience and moral sentiment can become diverse enough so that it becomes difficult to create unity. The state or government, developing along with the division of labour, helps to enforce the kind of discipline necessary to prevent the breakdown of institutions. But the requisite basis of comprehension and sentiment (understanding and identifying with the common, public interest in unity) is still lacking. The desire for unity, as well as obligation, must be present.

In some highly specialized occupations, we become more detached. Specialization increases, enterprises and markets grow in size, there is a lack of close contact between functions, and employer/employee relations become strained. For Durkheim, "[t]hese new conditions of industrial life naturally demand a new organization, but as these changes have been accomplished with extreme rapidity, the interests in conflict have not yet had the time to be equilibrated" (370).

Although the state (a spontaneous outgrowth of functional differentiation in Durkheim's view) has had some success in regulating conflict, the sentiment that all are working on a common, public project is still lacking. The state can moderate competition but not suppress it. Even in the case of organic solidarity, there must exist a cultural, symbolic basis for collective unity. In the case of rapid specialization, the rational and affective appreciation of the common goals involved is missing, and the state has difficulty in instilling it. "If the division of labour does not produce solidarity in all these cases, it is because the relations of the organs are not regulated, because they are in a state of *anomy*" (368). Workers must understand their purpose and willingly submit to the duties involved. The pathological state produced by rapid specialization is called the anomic division of labour.

Although it is Durkheim's belief that in a properly ordered and integrated society with a high differentiation of function each individual would be able to aspire to and achieve that position commensurate with his/her ability and potential, he also realizes that there are, at least some of the time, conditions which prevent this "equilibration." A "forced" division of labour is his name for the condition in which class or caste divisions permit the distribution of individuals to positions without regard for the "natural talents" of those individuals.

Durkheim and others use biological analogies to describe specialization of function. For example, as an organism develops, various cells differentiate to become part of brain tissue, bone tissue, muscle tissue, etc. Although individuals in society adopt specialized functions in different institutions or enterprises, this is not bio-chemically determined, and

Durkheim recognizes the limited applicability of the biological analogy (374). The limits of the analogy become particularly evident when the emergence of a new specialization is considered.

In society, there is often a lack of correspondence between individual aptitudes and the activity assigned to individuals. External constraint makes this so. Labour is not spontaneously and equitably divided where the constraint of state regulation occurs on a class basis. On the contrary, "labour is divided spontaneously only if society is constituted in such a way that social inequalities exactly express natural inequalities" (377). Otherwise, external conditions in the form of class or caste inequality and regulation based on inequality prevent the equitable distribution of individuals to positions. Inherited wealth, quite simply, can create inequality of opportunity.

Considerations of status (position dependent on personally ascribed characteristics such as parentage) give way (following the dictum of Sir Henry Sumner Maine, status to contract) to considerations of contract. In Durkheim's view, it is the growth of the division of labour itself which tends eventually to level these inequalities (378).

> Contractual relations necessarily develop with the division of labour, since the latter is not possible without exchange, and the contract is the juridical form of exchange. In other words, one of the important varieties of organic solidarity is what one might call contractual solidarity. (381)

Conflict can still result from contracts, but contract law grows and takes over the function of assuring the smooth functioning of contractual relations. "Public conscience" regulates exchange so as to assure equal value to both parties. "It finds unjust every exchange where the price of the object bears no relation to the trouble it cost and the service it renders" (382-83). Just remuneration for work is a demand which, if unfulfilled, can be a source of conflict. To reduce this conflict, it is necessary that what Durkheim has called "external conditions" be made equal.

Under the heading "Another Abnormal Form" of the division of labour, Durkheim attempts to point out a general lack of coordination of productive means and activity. In this brief section, which calls to mind Marx's discussions of capital accumulation and crisis, he points to cyclical problems of un- and underemployment. If these conditions could be properly regulated and organized, solidarity, according to Durkheim, would be assured.

SOCIOLOGICAL METHOD

HAVING ALREADY carried out a major, systematic and empirical study with moral/political aims, Durkheim turned to a formal defense of the precepts and approach entailed in his notions of society and morality. He did this in *The Rules of Sociological Method* [1895](1938). Here he is at pains to confirm the existence of collective forces which do not emanate from the individual. In a claim reminiscent of Comte, Durkheim announces the urgent need to rid conceptions of social and collective matters of their anthropomorphism. Thus, he argues for the existence of a collective realm of facts, accessible by an appropriate method.

His primary purpose in this work, which Thompson (1982: 92) sees as more of a manifesto for the discipline of sociology than a practical guide to the conduct of concrete research projects, is to defend the specifically sociological enterprise against other disciplines and approaches which might raise a claim to offer explanations of the same phenomena. Philosophers and psychologists, for example, may have produced elegant and fruitful studies of the nature of the human being or of humanity but, even if these be general enough to be correct, Durkheim is more interested in the scientific study of the variation in and diversity of human thought and conduct. We must, according to Durkheim, seek the source of this variation in the varying collective representations and diverse forms of social organization.

Humans do not act the same way, and the differences in conduct cannot be understood on the basis of individuals choosing to behave differently. Although we may know some people for whom the world appears to be brand new each day, most of us engage in forms of conduct which, for Durkheim, are the result of *social facts*. He defines these social facts as "ways of acting, thinking and feeling, external to the individual, and endowed with a power of coercion, by reason of which they control him" (1938: 3). Individuals act, think, and feel, but the *ways* in which they do this are not their own invention. Social facts are imposed on individuals, hence they are external to them; they are very powerful and regulate their conduct. In fact, Durkheim would claim that, if there were completely open choice available to us, this situation would be threatening and damaging. We would be lost, not knowing which way to turn, and would engage in acts which would not satisfy our desires.

Durkheim's precepts, outlined briefly, are these:

1. the distinct object or subject matter of sociology is social facts;
2. social facts are external and constraining ways of acting, thinking and feeling;
3. social facts are rooted in group sentiments and values;
4. social facts are manifested in external indicators of sentiments such as religious doctrines, laws, moral codes, and aphorisms; and
5. although they are not material, social facts are to be considered as real things exerting a real force observable in real effects.

Social facts comprise a distinct subject matter because, as collective representations, they are independent of psychological and biological phenomena. Although we have individual actions, thoughts, and feelings, we tend to live our lives through institutions: family, corporation, church, school, and Friday nights at the pub. Whether we speak of the corporation or the pub, different though the feeling or atmosphere in each may be, our actions in each are nonetheless regulated; there are more or less strict norms for each and we tend to follow them, each of us in our own way.

These ways of acting, thinking, and feeling are external to the individual and exercise coercive power. Sanctions are imposed for attempting to resist them. Recall Durkheim's discussion of repressive law in *The Division of Labour*. Even where behaviours are not legally proscribed (crimes), stigmatization resulting from these behaviours can still severely limit one's opportunities for interaction with others and one's life chances in general.

Social facts are rooted in group sentiments, values, attitudes and beliefs. These sentiments which people have in common are the products of that group life. Love for the prophet Mohammed, defense of abortion on demand, of the anti-cult movement, or of free trade are not the result of individuals happening to have incurred similar stimulations of neural pathways, nor of having used the rules of formal logic. Rather these sentiments are a product of similar patterns of group affiliation and interactional rootedness such as family, religion, and education.

These basic assumptions, arguments, and precepts are Durkheim's justification for the establishment of sociology as an independent discipline. Social facts as Durkheim articulates them are ways of doing things and are external and coercive. They are also seen to be rooted in group sentiments, attitudes, and beliefs. Although social facts are the proper subject matter for sociology, if it is to be a science, it must have some more concrete, observable object to examine. We can observe neither the sentiments nor the collective representations rooted in them. We must infer these from systematic observation of a more external manifestation or indicator of them. What we can observe are these external indicators of sentiments and of ways of doing things, namely, religious doctrines, laws, and moral codes. Body temperature is an indicator of physiological processes, and thus helps provide biology and medicine with a systematic, scientific status and method; the indicators noted above do the same for sociology.

In order to proceed scientifically, first of all, we must "eradicate all preconceptions" (1938: 14). If we conceive of social facts or phenomena as preconceptions rooted in particular group sentiments, we shall fail to find the appropriate external indicator and hence miss the essential properties of the facts involved. We all have conceptions about objects such as plants, animals, or rocks in terms of their beauty, pleasantness, legends of their origin, usefulness to us, or status in the environmental movement. To study the regular, systematic properties of these objects, natural scientists must rid themselves of preconceptions. Preconceptions about the social world, the origin of sentiments and collective representations, are even more pervasive and difficult to counteract. We all have firmly established notions about what must be done about crime, immigration, free trade, unions, and military scandal. In order to study the regular properties of crime, and trade and industrial conflict, and their relation to other things, we must put aside our sentiments and preconceptions. It is precisely the focus on objective, external indicators, such as the religious doctrines or laws mentioned above, which provides this objectivity.

We must also be able to generalize. If we want to make claims about the nature of social solidarity, it will not do to look only at its mechanical forms, those forms extant in more archaic societies as well as in more communal sub-groups in modern societies. We must attempt to look at all forms of a given class of phenomena and find the external indicators of the social facts producing them.

The phenomena, for their part, may be seen rather simply as people doing things. But people tend to do things according to rules. The rules, in turn, are ways of thinking, acting, and feeling, rooted in group sentiments and observable in laws, doctrines, codes, and organizational forms. For example, people engage in multiple acts of exchange and, on occasion, become involved in disputes over exchanges. People do these things, furthermore, as the result of their organized relations with one another and of the rules produced as collective representations.

Organized relations and the regulation of these relations, thus, are the cause of such interactions. The advancing division of labour and the concomitant relations of interdependent interactions cause exchanges, exchange disputes, and exchange dispute-resolution. The cause of a phenomenon, for Durkheim, is to be distinguished from its function, and we are to seek them separately. The cause of a social phenomenon is to be sought in terms of an antecedent social fact (independent variable in the language of modern methodology) and the function is to be sought in terms of a consequent social fact (dependent variable). The antecedent social fact in the above example is the advanced division of labour and resulting interdependence. The consequent social fact is the set of rules governing exchange disputes in contract law and the everyday moral codes which tend to produce a feeling of solidarity in pursuing common, public goals.

If I sell you my car for an agreed price of $950 (this, alas, reflects the state of a theory instructor's vehicle), and we live in a condition where our means of transport are not self-provided, and, furthermore, our agreement stipulates that after an initial payment of $450 you agree to two additional monthly instalments of $250, the second of which does not appear to be forthcoming, I may take you to small claims court for the remaining $250 (plus costs). The causes of this phenomenon are the advanced division of labour wherein means of transport are produced by specialists and exchanged, and the contract laws regulating exchange behaviour. These causes constitute the antecedent social fact.

The consequent social fact, the social function, comprises the feelings of solidarity in members and the maintenance of orderly relations. Imagine what might ensue if it were possible for anyone to welch on the $250 owing, mentioned above. What effects might this have? It is helpful to engage in such thought experiments to understand what Durkheim had in mind by his notions of social cause and social effect.

There are two general kinds of social phenomena, normal and pathological (morbid). The normal, for Durkheim, are those which are most widely distributed. They would not be the most common or widely distributed phenomena, he argues, if they did not contribute to the maintenance of society. Recall that Durkheim began his studies in moral philosophy, hoped to develop a science of ethics, and wanted a stronger, more unified France. The continued existence of normal phenomena illustrates their usefulness. They serve to maintain that which causes them. A social organism possessing a fairly wide distribution of pathological phenomena, on the other hand, would have difficulty surviving. Note that the normal can only be defined with reference to a particular society at a particular stage of its development. If Durkheim could identify the general characteristics of pathological phenomena, of social problems and ills, he might enable a scientific approach to the social reconstruction of French society. By turning his analytical attention to a particularly pathological phenomenon, suicide, Durkheim connects concerns raised in *The Division of Labour* with his theoretical and methodological assumptions and hopes, thereby flesh out his entire methodology of cause, effect, and remedy.

SUICIDE

In *Suicide*, his next project, Durkheim firmly established the method and discipline outlined in *Rules*. He applied these methods to a phenomenon which most would have taken to be the quintessentially individual act. Individuals can be seen as having "reasons" for the act of suicide, but Durkheim wanted to establish sociological factors as capable of explaining much about such anti-social phenomena. While there may be any number of individual reasons, Durkheim noticed that in some societies it appears that more individuals have such reasons than in others. In other words, sociology could explain differences in *rates* of suicide and perhaps indicate the sociological factors responsible for causing more individuals to respond with such finality to the presence of these factors.

Durkheim noticed that rates of suicide appeared to vary from country to country. Since there appeared to be a different "predisposition to suicide" in different societies,

Durkheim took up the task of finding out what caused this predisposition. The various individual reasons for suicide did not seem capable of explaining differences in rates, so he searched for an extra-individual, social explanation.

The method Durkheim used was to eliminate, one by one, the possible non-social explanations. Some kinds of suicide might be related to mental illness, but since not all kinds could be accounted for by this factor, it failed to explain the collective tendency which the statistics displayed. These statistics represented an external indicator of internal states. With what other social fact(s) might this be related? It did display a relation with age (the older, the more likely), but not with alcoholism. External, non-social factors, such as geography or climate were also ruled out. As one surveys the figures for Europe, the highest rates are in the middle; in each country, most suicides occur in the warmest months. Searching through the various individual motives, he decided, would not help to explain the collective tendencies.

In his search for a social factor, he noticed other statistical variations which might point to underlying social causes. Two of these are gender and religion. For example, he noticed that in Austria in the years 1873-77, 11,429 men had committed suicide compared to only 2,478 women. Similarly, in France (1871-76) 25,341 men and 6,839 women and in England (1863-67) 4,905 men and 1,791 women had apparently ended their lives at their own hand. Although these figures do not provide us with a suitable basis for comparing national rates (we do not have a necessary population base and do not know that the data was collected by the same criteria), there is nonetheless a rather striking difference in the rates according to gender. Durkheim wondered how these gender differences might point to underlying social causes. How might the collective lives of men and women be different so as to account for the different tendency to suicide?

In the case of religion as an indicator, two examples display some interesting differences. In Switzerland, in 1876, 87 German Catholics, 293 German Protestants, 83 French Catholics, and 456 French Protestants committed suicide.

Although we would want to know the relative populations of these four groups, these figures may suggest that religion could be an indicator, an external manifestation, of an underlying social fact. In a somewhat more refined presentation of data, Durkheim listed suicides per million population in societies with varying religious composition: Protestant 190, mixed 96, Catholic 58, and Greek Catholic 40. Remember that these figures are per 1,000,000 population, and as long as the time periods are quite similar, they would seem to suggest that religious affiliation and membership could indicate something about the conditions affecting suicide rates.

Although Durkheim has already mentioned religious doctrines as external indicators of the group sentiments which are, in turn, the root of social facts, ways of life, there is another feature of religious doctrine in need of examination in connection with the phenomenon of suicide. Some religions have doctrines specifically prohibiting suicide. Catholic doctrine, for example, expressly forbids the burial in a Catholic cemetery of anyone who has committed suicide. Since Protestant doctrine contains no such proscription, Perhaps this alone could explain the Catholic/Protestant variation. But this proves inadequate as an explanation when one realizes that Jewish doctrine contains the same proscription against suicide found in Catholic doctrine; yet, the Jewish rate is significantly lower than the Catholic. Since specific doctrine cannot explain this difference, Durkheim decided to look elsewhere for the cause. Of course, doctrinal differences do not explain the gender variation.

There is something else, however, about the difference between Catholic and Protestant doctrine which, according to Durkheim, might lead us in a more fruitful direction. During the Protestant Reformation, traditional beliefs had been overthrown; the individual's relation with God was emphasized and, subsequently, the role of communally practised rites, sacraments, and regulated contact amongst parishioners declined in significance. Luther had translated the Bible into the vernacular to enable a more individualistic orientation to faith. Catholics, on the other hand, can experience normally regulated contact with one another through the Church. In the case of Jews, argues Durkheim, the systematic oppression which they have endured creates an even more solid community. In fact, Durkheim notes lower suicide rates for minority groups.

How might this normative, institutional regulation be related to the gender difference? According to Durkheim, just as the Protestant may tend to lead a more individualistic, atomized existence, so, generally, do men, especially those in commercial and industrial occupations. In traditional family life, it tended to be the women whose lives were more normatively regulated, especially where this life involved caring for others. One is less likely to commit suicide where relations with others are governed by strong everyday norms which reinforce familial obligations. Whether work-related, religious, educational, or family-related, one's satisfactions are more attainable where norms place limits on individual tendencies. When responsibility for the welfare of others is involved, suicide is even less likely. Even men are less likely to commit suicide, if they have children.

Durkheim claims that the most fundamental factor affecting suicide rates is a breakdown of the integration of a community or society. Where there are strong, consensual norms, everyday rules regulating the conduct and interaction of persons in various institutional spheres, the rate of suicide will be low. The condition in which there is a lower degree of integration, where norms have broken down, is that condition which Durkheim calls *anomie*, normlessness. In this condition, individuals experience a lack of regulation of conduct, weaker ties with others, a lack of limits on tendencies and desires, and a lack of satisfaction generally.

Durkheim's discovery that the normative regulation of conduct and interaction had a precise role in affecting suicide rates led him to classify suicide into four types: egoistic, altruistic, anomic, and fatalistic. He identified as *egoistic* that kind of suicide where the individual chooses to ignore norms which are in fact characteristic of the individual's community of origin. S/he may, however, assert an individual preference to abandon those norms, perhaps for the purpose of seeking private gain, "fame and fortune." If the resultant gain is subsequently lost, as, for example in the famous 1929 stock market crash, and the shame of both the loss and rejection of original norms prevents a return to them, the individual may opt for suicide. Suicide can also result, claims Durkheim, from too strong an integration. This kind is usually military in context, such as practices of Hari Kiri, where the Samurai's honour is at stake. The individual dies, in essence, for the society, and Durkheim thus calls this kind of suicide *altruistic*. He labels *anomic* the kind of suicide resulting from the breakdown of the norms themselves. In some professions, isolation from others is characteristic and under conditions of rapid social change, suicide rates will be higher. Rapid processes of growth and modernization may tend toward the breakdown of social norms, thus leaving many individuals in that less-than-regulated state referred to as anomie. Remember that the division of labour is, in Durkheim's terms, not itself responsible for this breakdown; it is Durkheim's project to attempt to articulate the measures to be taken which will restore the required degree of normative regulation to prevent these higher occurrences of anti-social phenomena. Lastly, he also identified a kind of suicide called *fatalistic*, which could result from the existence of too many norms to follow. Where regulations are too numerous to allow comfortable integration, some individuals may experience too much pressure from this constant requirement and "opt out."

SOCIOLOGY, MORALITY, EDUCATION, AND RELIGION

In *Moral Education*, a book not published until 1925, after Durkheim's death, and likely taken from lecture notes for courses delivered between 1889 and 1912 in both Bourdeaux and Paris (see Lukes 1973: 110), he sets out most clearly his view of the place of sociology in investigating and reforming society and thought. It is in this work that he develops and makes known his project to make public the knowledge of the substantial, rational, and real basis of morality. According to Durkheim, educational institutions are capable of communicating the truly rational foundation for morality in the wake of the decline of religion. In other words, members' knowledge of the real basis of morality will allow them to engage in it willingly. Moral forces formerly expressed only in the terms of religion must be explained, and this explanation used as the basis for rational assent and compliance.

Moral ideas and sentiments are to be retained, but the historical bond with religion must be broken, and a new one, between educational institutions and the wider society, forged. To accomplish this, we must understand the genuine nature of morality and then indicate its development and orientation for current conditions. The term "moral", for Durkheim, has nothing to do with human nature; the term refers to collective ties and bonds. Morality has to do with duty, with prescribed behaviours. Regular, reliable, and dependable patterns of conduct are at issue.

Although Durkheim's notion of *homo duplex* indicates that drives and norms are opposing tendencies, drives pulling the individual in one direction and norms in, perhaps, the opposite one, his attention was focused on the possible harmonizing of the two. The satisfaction of drives and urges, the components of individual consciousness, demands, by definition, that these drives be limited. Infinite drives are *ipso facto* insatiable. It is the demands of collective, moral authority which provide limits and thus make individual satisfaction possible. When individual desires are controlled in this way by collective authority, not only is satisfaction possible, but common goals are also enabled in this process. Thus, Durkheim states, "[w]ill is formed in the school of duty" (1961: 46).

Historically, it had been the case that the collective assent required by such authority was achieved by religious means. But in more advanced societies, the effect of religious authority was less automatic. As religion declines, the role of society as the source and object of moral goals becomes clearer. The *real* moral being is society, not divine or supernatural beings, argues Durkheim. Under these new conditions, sociology and secular morality are interdependent; a conception of the whole as greater than the sum of its parts is necessary, not only for understanding morality, but for producing a harmonious version of it.

Also under such conditions, the individual will becomes much more reflective, less blindly faithful. There thus emerges a collectively, historically-produced intellect, capable of understanding the real, empirical foundations of the very morality which will provide him/her with appropriate satisfactions and common goals. While individual discipline is necessary to limit desires and thus enable satisfaction, attachment to social groups is the moral good involved and is the means by which discipline becomes possible. In the past, morality has had an "air of ideal transcendence"; this air of transcendence has usually been interpreted as having a divine, religious basis. Sociology enables us to see that this transcendent character belongs to society and we can now strip away from morality its mythical forms.

Science, Durkheim argues, is the heir of religion (in fact, it also has religious origins), and the modern, reflective intellect can use science to provide authority for moral compliance. The authority behind discipline is the group of attachment. Morality, thus, is made for society by society. Social structure, for Durkheim, produces morality. Durkheim claims, in fact, to be able to deduce the characteristics of a society's organization from knowledge of marriage patterns and family morals. The organizational deficiencies preventing moral harmony and solidarity, for Durkheim, are the decline in religious institutions and the failure of the social structure to provide new institutions to pick up the slack in this area.

Since a rational rather than a mythical basis for solidarity and morality is now possible, Durkheim suggests that education, and scientific education in particular, is key to a reflective, intellectual, and scientific basis for solidarity. Rapid change has made this sort of intervention necessary. While the family is self-sufficient, the nation requires a school. Morality, he argues, is not impoverished by being expressed in rational terms. Whereas traditionally the deity has been the symbolic expression of the basis of morality, it has also been the symbolic expression of the collectivity. Since we are now capable of rationally understanding this basis and this process, we can now teach that this basis is necessary and useful and, thus, provides the foundation for informed assent. Assent is thus produced through an understanding of its true causes.

The main purpose of Durkheim's educational reform is to induce a rational understanding of the moral order. When we know the reasons for morality, we are not under constraint. We can master the moral world through science because science has enlightened us about the rational basis for the moral imperative. Discipline and attachment to social groups comprise the first two elements of morality; the third element is the understanding of the nature of morality. Thus, for Durkheim, increasing our understanding of morality is itself a moral endeavour. Our understanding of the real basis and reasons for moral order is the best foundation for moral order. In order to understand, we require a scientific, sociological education. Intervention in the form of education is necessary due to the lack of intermediate groups (see discussion of *Division of Labour* above) such as provinces, communes, and guilds. Durkheim blames the abolition of these on the French Revolution. The school, therefore, provides not only an intermediate group, supplying norms for those involved in it, but also provides the entire nation with a rational, informed basis for national morality and solidarity.

Science, which in Durkheim's terms grew out of religion as the human intellect developed on a collective basis, also turns out to "give back something", as it were, to the source which made it thrive. Scientific understanding of the true, real, collective, social bases of moral order, assent, and the understanding of the necessity for both, can produce an enlightened compliance to a new, necessary moral order.

SCIENCE AND RELIGION
– AUTHORITY AND SOCIETY

I N *Primitive Classification*, Durkheim and Mauss set out to relativize logic and thought. They succeeded in doing this to a point. They relativized thought to society; they argued for its social and historical specificity. They came, however, to see the form of thought or logic evident in their own discipline and society as relatively autonomous and superior, but as resting on the base provided by earlier forms.

Whereas the modern discipline of logic supposes that particular operations of the human mind have transcendent and ahistorical foundations, Durkheim and Mauss, in noticing that different peoples think differently, suggested that the way a people thinks, classifies things in the world, has something to do with the way they live. (Notice the anti-Enlightenment cast to this notion. Instead of a universal, fundamentally equipped human mind, we have socially and historically-specific minds.) Specifically, the way people are organized in society, in terms of group affiliation and function, determines the way the society's members classify the things of nature.

Logic, for Durkheim and Mauss, has a history. This kind of statement can be supported by the fact that, given any collection of things, we can group these things according to similarities in any number of ways; they can be grouped by the kinds of features they exhibit or by their dimensions if these are thought to be similar. A large collection of, say, animals, can be grouped according to their position in some evolutionary scheme, according to how many legs they have, whether they have moveable ears, or whether they live in water, on land, or in the air. Thus expressed, classification schemes appear to be rather arbitrary. But, according to Durkheim and Mauss, they certainly are not arbitrary. Any collection of objects can, in principle, be classified in any way; the question is: "How did a given group of people classify things?" Durkheim and Mauss' answer is that they did this according to a template or foundation provided by the organizational form of their society.

By looking at so-called "primitive" classification, they believed that they had achieved access to some primordial form of logic. While this is at least questionable and the use of terms like "primitive" have recognizably pernicious connotations, Durkheim and Mauss are, nonetheless, making a cogent point about the historical specificity of forms of thought. Logic is essentially a classification scheme, and the scheme can take different forms. What factor(s) determines these forms?

One clue to the social basis of classification schemes is the fact that the Greek word "genos", kind, originally meant family, kin. It now comes to mean kind, "genus," in our modern biological system of classification. In fact, Durkheim and Mauss investigated, according to available ethnographic data, the possible kin or clan basis of classification categories. The best example of this is their discussion of the Zuñi.

The Zuñi divide the world into seven regions: north, west, south, east, zenith, nadir, and centre. The clans which make up the society are grouped into the various regions. The animals and plants, furthermore, after which the clans are named, are also grouped into those regions. The north corresponds to war, the west to hunting, the south to agriculture, and the east to religion. These regions are seen to take these correspondences from the functions of the clans grouped in them; the animals from which the clans take their names are also seen to perform similar, related functions in the operation of nature, pelicans in the north, bears in the west, badgers in the south, and deer in the east.

Social, moral authority is the basis of this kind of scheme for Durkheim and Mauss. They see social organization based on group affiliation and function as the basis or template on which conceptions, mythologies, and explanations of nature are founded. This authority operates so as to keep the society going. Thus, members of particular clans see the performance of these functions and duties as obedience to a divinely-inspired rule; if they deviate from these patterns, both they and their society are in trouble. Society ensures our compliance by producing convincing interpretations of nature and of our place in it. While the clan member sees

these interpretations as having a religious or mythical foundation, the sociologist refers them to their basis in social
organization and the authority which this organization produces. This represents human society's first and basic attempt
to make intelligible the relations which exist between things,
and it provides the foundation for more advanced attempts.

In *The Elementary Forms of The Religious Life*, Durkheim
believed that he had found an appropriate starting point for
the analysis of religion; he also thought he had discovered
the relation between collective authority and the sacred. Although he did not believe that one could scientifically investigate the question of the actual origin of religion, he,
nonetheless, felt that one could view extant forms of religious thought and practice which did not exhibit the centuries or millennia of subsequent layers of "secondary
characteristics" displayed by more advanced religious forms
(1965: 20-21). What he called totemic belief systems present
the investigator with a kind of experimental control, a "primitive" belief system without subsequent divisions and institutions whose effects might also be present and prevent our
direct observation of fundamentally religious phenomena.

No religion, understood by Durkheim as a system of collective representations, could be false (1965: 15). Such systems must have "worked" in order to have persisted at all.

> [I]t is an essential postulate of sociology that a human
> institution cannot rest upon an error and a lie, without
> which it would not exist. If it were not founded in the
> nature of things, it would have encountered in the facts
> a resistance over which it could never have triumphed.
> (1965: 14)

Durkheim, remember, is a rationalist. For him, scientific approaches are preferable to religious ones. However, it cannot
be denied that religion has been a real phenomenon and a
real force in human life. Also, since so many peoples acted
for so long on the basis of so many diverse and, to the modern
eye, such wondrous, beliefs and belief systems, it is unlikely

that centuries-long ways of life and ideas could be utterly false and fantastic. Believers could produce goods, keep order, and explain rather complex events all on the basis of what Durkheim is here referring to as "primitive" or "totemic" beliefs. For Durkheim, "totemic" beliefs are not the best way of understanding nature, society, or anything else: they are, nonetheless, extraordinarily important and deserve close study for what they might tell us about the basis of knowledge and understanding.

> The most barbarous and the most fantastic rites and the strangest myths translate some human need, some aspect of life, either individual or social. The reasons with which the faithful justify themselves may be, and generally are, erroneous; but the true reasons do not cease to exist, and it is the duty of science to discover them. (1965: 14-15)

Although Durkheim is unwilling to accept a believer's justification, he, nonetheless, thinks that there are "real" reasons for such commitments. The ways in which people have typically "pictured to themselves the world and themselves" have a religious origin and character. It is fairly recently in our history that our understanding has taken on anything other than a religious form. Rationalist and scientific endeavours have historical roots in their religious predecessors. "If philosophy and the sciences were born of religion, it is because religion began by taking the place of the sciences and philosophy" (1965: 21). Although by "place of the sciences and philosophy," Durkheim means something like "functional place," this signals a rather Eurocentric, rationalist position. Earlier thinkers like Edward Tylor and Herbert Spencer displayed similar prejudices in imagining that "primitives" devised fantastic beliefs because they were forced to reason with fewer resources than their modern counterparts. To some extent, Durkheim exhibits the same behaviour, but he also states that other belief systems possess their own logic. Different logics are rooted in different societies; "religion is something eminently social" (1965: 22).

In formulating these major questions, Durkheim anticipates his conclusion when he states:

> It is the very authority of society, transferring itself to a certain manner of thought, which is the indispensable condition of all common action. The necessity with which the categories are imposed on us is not the effect of simple habits whose yoke we could easily throw off with a little effort; nor is it a physical or metaphysical necessity, since the categories change in different places and times; it is a special sort of moral necessity which is to the intellectual life what moral obligation is to the will. (1965: 30)

In Durkheim's view, religious belief and practice are fundamental to the formation of the human intellect. Religion did not simply contribute a few ideas or representations now and then but played a role in actually shaping the intellect itself. In other words, the categories, the frameworks or "lenses" we employ for picturing, understanding, and moving about in the world have a religious origin.

The categories of space, time, and causality, for example, the means by which people classify, arrange, and make sense of the things in their world, have a social, religious origin. Though fundamentally religious in character, they also have a specificity in connection with the particular society in which they are found and employed. If we find someone employing a category of time, we will find others in that society using it as well. Time is divided into days, weeks, months, or years, as the case may be, based on the recurrence of festivals and rites. Astronomical or climactic phenomena may also be used as a marker for these, but their significance and meaning derive from the patterns of social life and the authority of the whole which underlies them. Divisions of space have parallel origins (see the example of the Zuñi above).

But the distinction most fundamental to religious phenomena is that between the sacred and the profane. Some modes of thought and action are properly religious in character because they pertain to sacred things. These take on an absolute and inviolable status. Other, non-sacred objects and practices are profane and are sharply demarcated from the sacred. This is the most fundamental division between the different things in the world.

It is religious beliefs or representations which ascribe sacred status to particular things. In addition to beliefs, there are rites which are "determinate modes of action" involving sacred objects defined by religious beliefs. Durkheim employs the example of initiation rites as an illustration. In many cultures, boys participate in initiation rites in order to pass into manhood. This passage, according to Durkheim, is a passage between two sharply separated worlds, the profane and sacred. The boy must undergo sacred procedures to effect this difficult passage and, as a result, may enjoy privileged contact with sacred objects and places. These procedures and statuses, among others, will, in turn, help to order and arrange the status and activity of other persons, objects, and activities in the society. Most importantly, in Durkheim's view, the sacred status around which things, persons, and actions are organized is due to social, moral authority. Religious beliefs serve to define the sacred for the purpose of guiding action in rites; thought guides action in the same manner. Collectively performed rites help "to excite, maintain or recreate certain mental states in these groups" (1965: 22). Beliefs and practices are religious where their authority involves a sacred status. They are ultimately social, for Durkheim, because beliefs and practices are in turn based on collective, moral authority.

Perhaps this can be made clearer by presenting an example of what Durkheim has been calling "totemism." "Totem" is originally an Ojibway term which has been applied by anthropologists to belief systems in all sorts of tribal societies. We may already be familiar with the notion of a "totem pole." On these objects, we find stylized images, often of animals. These are material emblems, symbols, of several different things. We find them not only on poles, but also on the lodges of members. They also may be used in other forms in rites. They are simultaneously symbols of clans, animals, and gods. Thus, they represent a group of people, an animal, and a divine being. How is it possible, Durkheim asks, for a single emblem to represent both god and society? His short answer to this question is: because they are the same thing. For members of these societies, it is the sacred character of these objects or the power of divine beings represented by them which makes understandable the specific order of the world and the necessity of our acting in it in certain prescribed ways.

Take the example of the Zuñi mentioned above. If I am, for example, a member of the deer clan, ascribed to the east in space, my typical function might be cultivating corn. This is meaningful and understandable to me because of mythologies articulating the origin of deer, the deer clan, how it is that deer came to have the appearance and behaviours they do, and probably specifying certain do's and don'ts with respect to my contact with deer (I probably am not allowed to eat them). There is likely an origin myth explaining how in mythical time a partly human ancestor had intercourse with an equally mythical deer, thus explaining how it is that I am a member of the deer clan, why real deer behave the way they do, and why I *must* cultivate corn. From time to time rites are also performed which reinforce all of this. Imagine what might result if I could decide to be a cultivator, hunter, or shaman at will. Assume, as well, that members of the bear clan, hunters, were allowed to make similar choices without compulsion. We might all starve, and our society might well fall apart. It is the force of social, moral authority which prevents this, according to Durkheim.

There are very strong forces making me fulfil my function. Given the traditional mythology, I experience this force as having a divine origin as explained in the story. Remember that, to Durkheim, God and society are identical. Whereas, for believers, the force is divine, for Durkheim, it is social. In fact, according to Durkheim, it is the clan itself (or the whole society) which is asserting the force on its members. Durkheim's view is that the clan or society is too complex a reality for members to decipher (a Eurocentric interpretation at best). Collective assemblies and rituals help reinforce the sense of obligation, but for believers obligation has divine origins. Religion, according to Durkheim, results from a case of mistaken identity. Societal forces are mistaken for a god; the forces are real, but misinterpreted. Society provides us with an understanding of nature and of the morally obligatory character of our actions within nature and society.

The human intellect and its ability to comprehend nature are initially shaped in this way. Without this initial development, no further evolution is possible. Upon this historical basis, human understanding assumes specialized forms. In tribal societies, nature is understood in religious terms. Priests or shamans have the most specialized roles, and their job is to interpret or on occasion to make things right. As the division of labour developed, the individual intellect was freed from this collectively obligatory condition. Just as individuality was made possible, in terms of occupation and personality, by the development of the division of labour, so did the individual intellect acquire the freedom to contemplate nature more or less "on its own." Today, we are no longer bound to collectively held notions of nature. Originally, a concept of nature would be taken to be true because it was collectively held; now it only becomes collectively held after being proven to be true (1965: 485-86). In other words, the position of scientist is a specialized branch of the division of labour owing a long history to both original understandings of nature and to the development of the division of labour.

Durkheim viewed himself as helping to tear off the mythological veil which had covered the real forces and conditions at issue. His primary project, remember, was to provide a sociological analysis of essential features of collective life. He believed that we can begin to understand and rationally appreciate the moral obligations necessary in modern society. It is this project which unifies his work.

4

Max Weber
(1864-1920)

MAX WEBER was a German polymath who excelled in many different fields including sociology, economics, history, law, jurisprudence, and linguistics. He displayed scholarly brilliance at an early age, quickly learned other languages as these provided access to materials helpful in his investigations, and pursued topics which were all over the intellectual, geographic, and historical map. The topics he examined ranged from Polish farm workers to ancient religions and medieval entrepreneurs.

Weber was born in Erfurt, in 1864, into a prominent family of industrialists and civil servants. His mother was a pious Protestant woman. His father was a lawyer, a member of the German parliament, and was well-connected to prominent intellectual, industrial, and political figures in Berlin, where the family moved when Weber was five. Although well-connected, his father, by all accounts, was rather shallow and did not treat his mother very well. This last trait caused conflict between Weber and his father and resulted in the younger Max throwing his father out of the house, shortly after which the latter died of a stroke. These events were to have prolonged effects on Weber's own mental and physical health, including a five-year period during which he spent his time recuperating and travelling. In 1892, he married Marianne Schnitger, a scholarly interlocutor in her own right, who was most supportive of Weber's career and hosted many prominent intellectuals of the day in Heidelberg, just as Weber's parents had in the Berlin of his youth.

Weber was trained in law and received his Ph.D. in that discipline in 1889 for a dissertation on medieval business organizations. He proceeded to complete a Habilitationsschrift on Roman agrarian history and was thus eligible to hold a university post. His first was at Freiburg, and two years later, he moved to Heidelberg. His last was at Munich.

The Germany of Weber's youth had rapidly industrialized, and this had left the country in a chaotic state with several constituencies vying for prominence in the setting of national, political agendas. Prussian Junkers (militaristic landowners) from the old regime, new industrialists, and their recently proletarianized workers all represented forces contending for influence in shaping modern Germany. Although national unity and cohesion were important to Weber, he was quite pessimistic, unlike Durkheim, about the chances of finding some broadly based consensus, rational or otherwise, upon which to ground this cohesion. He preferred to pursue studies and policy discussions which might contribute to conflict resolution because he feared the dominance of either the right or of the socialists and was less than impressed with the ineffective compromises of the National Liberals. He was also much more directly involved than Durkheim in everyday political questions and events. He even ran, although unsuccessfully, for office.

His many writings on social and economic organization, religion, science, and politics rarely appeared as books during his lifetime. Some of them were inspired by the pressing conflicts of his day, even though many of them were historical in character. Some studies were published in journals, such as *Archiv für Sozialwissenschaft und Sozialpolitik* (Archive for Social Science and Social Policy), and others appeared in collected volumes on topics such as the sociology of religion and the theory of science. His magnum opus is a two volume work entitled *Economy and Society*. He died of pneumonia in 1920.

According to Weber, the economic order was of paramount importance in determining the precise position of different communities, but other factors, under appropriate conditions, could influence people's action in ways not directly derivable from purely "economic" interests. Although, like Marx, he considered the economic order to be central, he thought that rational bureaucracy, rather than class struggle, was the most signficant factor in its current fuctioning, since the former determined individual, communal, and societal action in the modern condition.

In the words of Gerth and Mills (1946: 50), he was a nostalgic liberal. "Weber thus identifies bureaucracy with rationality, and the process of rationalization with mechanism, depersonalization, and oppressive routine. Rationality, in this context, is seen as adverse to personal freedom." The type of person found in public life is, in Weber's view, shaped in these processes of mechanization and bureaucratization. Gerth and Mills (1946: 50) nicely summarize his view of this person. He is:

> The narrowed professional, publicly certified and examined, and ready for tenure and career. His craving for security is balanced by his moderate ambitions and he is rewarded by the honor of official status. This type of man Weber deplored as a petty routine creature, lacking in heroism, human spontaneity, and inventiveness. The Puritan willed to be the vocational man that we have to be.

In fact, Weber had ambivalent feelings about rationality and bureaucracy. They made for a more efficient and precise attainment of institutional goals, yet, at the same time, restricted the real choices of real people as to the goals deemed worthwhile and the means available for their achievement. All forms of culture in the modern West from music to religion are subject to this trend. Weber wanted to know how rational bureaucracy, industrial capitalism, and modern science arose, and he attempted to base his answer on forms of social action and how these changed.

Weber employed ideal types of action, compared these to actual historical instances, and focused on the unintended consequences of action as these helped to produce change. As we shall see near the end of this chapter, the Puritan intention to serve God was enacted in such a way that it had the unintended consequence of providing the disciplined habits necessary for industrial capitalism. By comparing the grounds and consequences of action in different historical contexts, Weber was able to compare outcomes, actions, and structures in terms of common and unique features. By noting the effect of unique features on social action, Weber was able to approximate a meaningful and causal account of important historical developments. One could, he thought, achieve a causal explanation of results by isolating the key feature in two or more cases. For example, certain factors in civilizations other than Protestant Europe "blocked the emergence of capitalism" (Gerth and Mills 1946: 61).

Perhaps the clearest statement of his position appears in "Politics as a Vocation," a lecture delivered in 1918, in which Weber reiterates many of the major points made in the corpus of his scholarship. He argues that questions of politics are most readily answerable in terms of the position of officials and in terms of the possibilities for action which these positions enable or restrict. Politics, in this case, means, for Weber, leadership of a state where the state is defined as having a *"monopoly of the legitimate use of physical force* within a given territory" (Weber 1946: 78).

Whereas the state is the source of the right to use violence, politics is the attempt to share or redistribute this power. This definition raises the question: How it is that people accept domination by others as legitimate? The answer, fundamentally, deals with the status of tradition/habits, personalities, and rules. Historically, we have moved from traditional forms of authority and legitimacy; "charismatic" leaders and movements provided a means of change from time to time.

Whoever controls the means of administration (getting others to follow orders and carry out tasks) in the form of food, material, or weapons must form the necessary arrangements with others for the successful maintenance of power and order. Historically princes, warlords, or other power-holders have secured the allegiance of others who owned their own means of administration. Of crucial historical importance is the question of whether power-holders themselves direct an administration of either officials or confidants who do not themselves own the means. They can count on legitimacy (tradition, personal qualities, rules) to some extent but must also distribute rewards and social honour. These could be salaries, employee of the month awards, prebends (granting a position which entitles the holder to sources of income traditionally flowing to the holder of that position; fiefs and benefices also fit this general description), or the spoils of war. These kinds of relations have advantages (for power-holders) over other arrangements where a power-holder might have to maintain constant favourable contact with another power-holder, who owns his own means, for cooperation. Louis XIV could command those to whom he gave tax-farming rights. Charlemagne could not command those from whom he needed military cooperation. Today, the salaried employee and proletarian are separated from the means of administration. Politicians today often make their living as politicians. There may also be prebends involved, although these would be the stuff of a good tabloid exposé. Ultimate command does not rest with those who do not own the means of administration. The struggle for patronage becomes pervasive, and political parties have administrative leaders as well as political leaders and staff.

Political idealism is the luxury of those who have least to lose, and while this idealism, when expressed at the proper moment and embodied in the right leader might lead to communal action, the ethic of its absolute ends comes into conflict with what Weber calls the ethic of responsibility. Fervour for a particular goal which allows the right leader to draw a following requires that leaders secure from bureaucratic organizations the means to put up the good fight. Securing the means and "taking care of one's people" take their toll on the movement's idealism. Bureaucratic domination proves to be an excellent means for maintaining the sway of powerful interests.

In Weber's view, we inhabit a world where the satisfaction of interests and needs on the part of the majority of a population works almost perfectly to maintain the rule of vested, powerful groups. Certainly, in the past, there were those in power who had rather effective control over the distribution of rewards both economic and social. But there were other forces, some religious for example, at play in these situations. Splinter groups with heroic leaders armed with emotionally charged doctrines posed a more serious threat to those in power, especially if the ruled were suffering.

The modern condition presents a picture in which the vast majority of us adopt "realistic" goals and calculate systematically the appropriate means of achieving them. We have a "bottom line" and systematically consider the various conditions and choices that may affect it. The conditions and forces which may have a bearing can be calculated, and we can receive training in these general methods of calculation: bookkeeping, management science, human resource management, and linear optimization. The forces which are seen to matter are susceptible to this sort of systematic, calculating treatment. Commitment to any other sort of goal where the means may not be seen as calculable is itself seen as irrational. This is what Weber means by the term "rationalization." Much of his work is oriented to uncovering the process of its development.

APPROACH AND ASSUMPTIONS:
A SOCIOLOGICAL READING
OF HISTORY

WEBER HAD highly ambivalent feelings about these specifically modern, western developments. Western structures, thought, and action represent both advantages and disadvantages, in Weber's view. The development of bureaucracy, of capitalism, and of science are peculiarly western, and each embodies the western form of rationality. Science in particular, claims Weber (1958a: 13), tends to appear to us as a "cultural phenomenon of universal significance and validity." All spheres of culture tend to become rationalized, and it is this process of "rationalization" to which Weber attributes both positive and negative outcomes in terms of the possibilities for individual freedom.

All of Weber's inquiries into a wide variety of topics contribute to his answer to the question: How do phenomena such as bureaucracy, capitalist practices, and science arise? Other cultures had produced mathematics, empirical observations, medicine, rational philosophies, and systematic reflections on the conduct of life. But trained personnel in science and the state existed only in the modern West where organizations of all sorts are staffed by trained officials. Within the West, the state is run according to rational rules and laws governing the political, technical, and economic conditions of life. The outcomes of decisions and actions are made to be as calculable as possible.

Entrepreneurs tend to adjust their action to calculation in terms of capital. But the quest for ever-renewed profit which is the hallmark of capitalism cannot be reduced to a heightened acquisitive or greedy spirit. King Midas was not particularly modern. It is, rather, the modern constellation of structures and calculable goals which necessitates renewed profit to avoid complete ruin. There were profitable enterprises in earlier periods. But in the modern West, enterprises which satisfy almost all needs rationally organize free labour (Weber 1958a: 21). The control of formally free labour under capitalism is the crucial factor for Weber.

His investigation of the rise of these institutions and forms of life and conduct began with the kinds of action and organization found in his own society and culture. He formulated the types of action found there. Durkheim had been influenced philosophically by St. Simon, Comte, and their followers in France, and thus held the data of history to be more or less unproblematically extractable in the form of indicators of social facts. Whereas Weber, influenced by followers of Kant, such as Wilhelm Dilthey, Wilhelm Windelband, and Heinrich Rickert, held that the categories employed by the investigator (as opposed to those of the historical subjects) were formed by the values and culture of that investigator. What appears significant, interesting, meaningful, or objective in the subject matter (the object-of-knowledge in the Kantian sense) will be determined in part by the investigator's culturally-determined criteria of knowledge. Of course, this means that the distinction between facts and values becomes less clear since the facts themselves are seen as cultural productions of the social scientific investigator from his/her vantage point. Weber, nonetheless, made this distinction and suggested that although facts display a "value-relevance" or "relatedness to value," we can respect the otherwise important difference between them by resisting the temptation to derive "ought" from "is." Although facts, value-related though they are, can inform policy decisions, we cannot logically employ them as an absolute ground for claiming what should exist or be done.

> Each new fact may necessitate the re-adjustment of the relations between end and indispensable means, between desired goals and unavoidable consequences. But whether this re-adjustment *should* take place and what *should* be the practical conclusions to be drawn therefrom is not answerable by empirical science – in fact it cannot be answered by any science whatsoever. (Weber 1949: 23)

For example, if it is empirically determined that children in single-parent families have more emotional problems and lower school achievement, it does not scientifically or logically follow that divorce *should* be made illegal. Even though the significance and meaning of the facts are value-laden and culturally specific (their cultural meaningfulness is what allows us to "see" them in the first place and provide them with the status of objects-of-knowledge), there are still various and conflicting goals which we might want to achieve. But there is no scientific way of assessing the relative merits of conflicting goals. It is in this sense that Weber recommends that science remain ethically neutral. Discussions of value can suggest problems for investigation (1949: 21), but we cannot choose between them scientifically.

The rationality of modern science to which Weber held provided him with the perspective and means for analyzing various world-historical situations and events. He employed modern, western conceptions of rationality to see to what extent and in what ways other peoples' courses of action are similar or different, not to praise or condemn, but because this is the only way we have of making them understandable and explicable.

For Weber, to understand any social state of affairs or societal condition is to understand the actions of individual members therein. The economic order and the structure of institutional organizations are important considerations, but Weber's preference is for an account which begins and ends by considering people as they engage in daily activities within such orders and structures. We must begin with peoples' subjective motivations if we are to understand the action of individuals.

Objective histories may describe events, outcomes, and structures rather adequately and proceed to provide definitive accounts of legal, constitutional, economic, and constitutional arrangements. Weber, however, desired an account of life under such arrangements in terms of the motivations of the actions of individuals. His methodology, inasmuch as it may be called that, is designed to achieve precisely this. What things mean to individuals is an important motivating factor. Our actions with and toward things are based on what they mean to us. This is not fixed in the thing itself as a material object. Action is social when at least one of those "things" toward which we act is another person, and this action depends on particular actions on the part of that other.

To borrow one of Weber's examples, if we pick up an axe, we may be chopping wood for our fireplace, earning a wage, getting in shape, or venting rage. In each case a different subjective meaning is attached to the axe. Action is social when it takes into account other people. The conduct of others, in this case, is integral to the achievement of our objectives. Much of our conduct and its goals involve the actions of others and Weber was curious about the role of others' actions either as a means or as an end in our own action. In the case of the axe mentioned above, we may wonder whether the right tool and movement were selected given the four different motives or intentions discussed. How we conduct ourselves toward others, similarly, will affect whether the actions of others contribute to the achievement of our end or provide some obstacle to it.

In the real world, people are more or less competent members of communities and can usually handle an axe in some way or another which will allow them to make pieces of wood smaller with some degree of success. In the case of social action, the situation is somewhat more complicated. Members of communities often act *as* members of those communities. Such action makes these communities the precise communities that they are. This is not as trivial and obvious a point as it may at first appear. What is a typical labour union? What is a typical company? They are the typical actions of typical members. If we look around our world, present and past, we may find some interesting practices and institutions. We may also notice that practices, institutions, and conditions vary significantly from society to society and from era to era. A medieval guild and a modern union have some similarities and some differences. For Weber, an understanding of these similarities and differences necessarily entailed a grasp of what a guild member does and of what a union member does. A grasp of what either does, furthermore, entails an interpretive understanding of his/her actions. Guilds were common in the middle ages; therefore, we should be able to come up with a fairly reliable notion of what guilds were trying to do and of the typical results and consequences of their activities. To explain these results and consequences, we must first of all attempt to subjectively understand the motivations of guild members. We will be able explain the outcomes more or less successfully to the extent that the members' selection of means was appropriately made so as to bring about the realization of their ends. The ends must be rather common or typical or else we will have a hard time even imagining how one might go about achieving them.

In communities, organizations, and institutions, people accomplish all sorts of things. They often continue to accomplish similar sorts of things in the same ways. A university consists of students, professors, secretaries, janitors, librarians, administrators, and computer personnel. The actions of each are coordinated, and in Weber's view depend on a complex of meaning. All courses of action (going to lectures, giving lectures, passing exams, keeping departments together, cleaning blackboards, miraculously finding important material, and making one's self financially or technically indispensable) require coordination, in other words, everyone, in order to achieve his/her goal, must have a pretty good idea of everyone else's. The investigator must achieve "adequacy on the level of meaning": we must understand what the actions of each participant mean to the others, and how this affects their course of action. Once we have grasped this, and if there is a high likelihood that action in this sequence will take place again, then we have a causally adequate account as well. Weber calls his approach *Verstehen*, interpretive sociology.

This process may be relatively simple if we are examining courses of action with which we are intimately familiar. In historical cases, however, this process is more difficult, and it is this difficulty which primarily concerned Weber. In response, he constructed ideal types of action. The first type is "ideal" in the sense of being perfectly rational action, the selection of the most effective means for the achievement of an immediately practical goal or end. This describes purposive-rational action. If courses of action do not seem to follow this model, we must search for that factor (meaning) which produced a deviation from the rational. Weber is not maintaining that one should or must behave rationally; he is claiming, rather, that the comparative use of a rational ideal type is a good way of determining what motivates people in other cases. The other ideal types of action resulting from this theoretical analysis are traditional/habitual (simply following custom or habit; this may be action in Weber's sense only if it is rather self-conscious), emotional (based on gut feelings of anger, jealousy, or love, if self-conscious), and value-rational (attempting to maximize an absolute value, such as one might find in cultures with religious commandments for daily conduct).

Remember that Weber was attempting to understand how western European institutions and courses of action arose. To a large extent, he took rational, calculating westerners as a standard (ideal type) and attempted to locate the factors which prevented others from acting similarly. One will not find a pure case of any of the four kinds of action outlined above. These are employed for historical comparative purposes. We may, for example, find both economic *and* religious motivations for action in any particular case. His ideal types simply help him to apply precise concepts to particular historical cases and to investigate the real sources of people's actions.

ACTION, DOMINATION AND LEGITIMACY

E VEN THOUGH, for Weber, only individuals act, motives tend to converge. Some people are able to secure relatively willing compliance from others. Each of his four types of action corresponds roughly to a type of authority. Some, whose material and other advantages may be greater than those of their followers, are able to dominate others. Weber's term for this domination is "Herrschaft," literally, "lordship." Others have translated this variously as "domination," "authority," and "imperative coordination."

As with other ideal types, the pure types of authority or domination do not correspond perfectly with real cases, which most often involve a mixture of these types. In the majority of cases, argues Weber, the motives are qualitatively heterogeneous. If we are tempted, in the first place, to see action as motivated primarily by economic ends, we may expect its course to approximate the purely rational case. If it does not, the rationally pure type against which the actual case is compared may facilitate the search for non-economic motives (1978: 21). Similarly, if action is seen to be oriented, first and foremost, to mystical ends, it may be a good idea to see if there is any relation to political or economic affairs. These pure types enable precise analyses.

We can witness with greater clarity how ideal types operate for Weber by following his discussion of legitimate domination. Meaningful action and causal adequacy are made evident by means of analysis of ideal types. Domination is defined as the probability that commands will be carried out by a specific group of persons. This probability may be high for a number of reasons ranging from habit to the calculation of advantage. The obedient, according to Weber, have an interest in obeying.

Staff obey superiors by custom and for material advantage but a belief in legitimacy is also necessary. "[A]ccording to the kind of legitimacy which is claimed, the type of obedience, the kind of administrative staff developed to guarantee it, and the mode of exercising authority, will all differ fundamentally" (Weber 1978: 213). With each type of domination, a different claim to legitimacy is involved. There are three basic types of legitimate domination; for each, the claims to legitimacy are based on different grounds.

In the case of rational-legal authority the grounds are rational and rest "on a belief in the legality of enacted rules and the right of those elevated to authority under such rules to issue commands" (Weber 1978: 215). Traditional authority rests "on an established belief in the sanctity of immemorial traditions and the legitimacy of those exercising authority under them" (Weber 1978: 215). Charismatic grounds rest "on devotion to the exceptional sanctity, heroism or exemplary character of an individual person, and of the normative patterns or order revealed or ordained by him" (Weber 1978: 215). Obedience is thereby owed to an impersonal order, the person of the chief, or trust in exemplary qualities, respectively.

Weber begins with modern, rational-legal authority, the type we most readily understand since it is characteristic of our society, in order to contrast it with other types of authority and thereby render them more understandable. In order to understand a particular state of affairs, past or present, we must comprehend what brought this state of affairs into existence and what maintains it. We may want to know, as well, what possibilities exist for change in that state of affairs. Our historical development has been such that we exist in various communities of different size and interest. The actions of members tend to provide for the maintenance of the community or, in some cases, to give rise to a new community. Weber is interested in understanding these questions of origin and maintenance.

Communities are comprised of people occupying different positions. Those in certain positions (the highest) would usually prefer that the community and its position be maintained. Such goals demand the compliance of those in positions of less advantage, and Weber is at pains to describe how it is that such compliance is often forthcoming. He attempts to account for all of this in terms of action. One sort of act may be called a command. We attempt to understand this act, first of all, through the benefits accruing to the one voicing the command when those to whom the command is voiced, in fact, carry it out. Typically, the maintenance of some material benefit or privilege is at issue. The act called obedience, the high likelihood that the command will be carried out, on the other hand, may occur on a number of different grounds.

The most rational basis for obedience is a belief in the legitimacy of the rules entailed in the enactment of the command. But,the command may have been voiced by a person of a particular status, a status which traditionally entitles such a person to voice such commands. Or, the command may be voiced by an individual of such exemplary, heroic qualities that the reverence for those qualities provides an emotional ground for obedience. Here we have a brief description of rational-legal, traditional, and charismatic authority, respectively.

Purposive-rational action, finding the most appropriate, efficient means to the achievement of a given end, tends to be accompanied by rational-legal authority, grounded in legally established rules. Value-rational action, the maximization of an ultimate value in both the end sought and in the means selected, tends to be accompanied by traditional authority, authority grounded in revered traditions and in the appropriateness of those issuing commands. Emotional or affectual action, based on gut feelings, tends to be accompanied by charismatic authority grounded in loyalty to an individual possessing heroic qualities.

Weber defines domination in terms of the likelihood that commands will be carried out by a given group of persons. People thus have an array of motives (complexes of meaning) in complying voluntarily. They have an interest in obedience. Rulers, staff, and subjects have typical, understandable ends, and there is a high probability that actions toward those ends will, in fact, take place. The ends are thus legitimate, and we can analyze the motives for compliance with them. These motives may range, according to Weber (1978: 212), "from simple habituation to the most purely rational calculation of advantage." They may be ideal, material, affectual, or simply customary. The type of domination found will depend largely on the qualities of the motives. For any sort of domination to be stable, there must also exist a belief in its legitimacy. Again, Weber reminds us that he does not expect these types to exhaustively describe actual historical cases. They are intended to provide unambiguous concepts to allow historical comparisons.

RATIONAL-LEGAL AUTHORITY
AND BUREAUCRACY

WEBER BEGINS with the modern form of authority, rational-legal, and with the form of social organization which typically accompanies it, bureaucracy or bureaucratic administration. This type of authority typically manifests the following traits:

1. legal norms may be imposed or agreed upon;
2. there is a system of intentionally established, abstract rules (they are general and do not treat specific, concrete cases on their own merits);

3. superiors in authority are themselves subject to the impersonal order;
4. obedience to authority is by individuals as members of the organization, and members are obedient to the law; and
5. although the commands of persons are obeyed, obedience is owed to the impersonal order.

Official business is conducted according to rules, and specific jurisdictions are established with specified powers and means of compulsion. The organization is hierarchical, higher offices supervising lower ones. Rules are often technical, and training is required. Staff are separated from ownership of the means of production or of administration. Official positions are not appropriated. Written documents (files, memos) prevail; acts, decisions and rules are recorded.

Officials, holders of bureaucratic office, can be described by the following:

1. they are personally free (not bound to another person);
2. they are organized in a hierarchy of offices;
3. each has a clearly defined competence;
4. their office is contractually held;
5. technical qualifications determine their selection;
6. they are salaried;
7. their office is the primary occupation;
8. they have a career; the incumbent is expected to "move up";
9. the official owns neither the position nor the means of administration in any other sense; and
10. the official is subject to discipline in the conduct of office.

This pure type of rational-legal authority with its (purely) bureaucratic administration is generally capable, according to Weber, of efficiency, precision, and fairness. Results are calculable and predictable, and the high degree of impersonality has a levelling effect on status considerations. The ends of action are legitimate, commands are issued, and leaders and followers alike achieve expected outcomes as the result of purposive-rational action. Actions of various persons are coordinated in an impersonal and calculated way. This situation is rational in the sense of what Weber calls "formal rationality." Bureaucracies operate according to universally applicable rules or methods of procedure and, thus, pay little attention to differences between individual persons or matters of principle. If we were systematically to consider persons and cases on their merits, we would be engaging in "substantive rationality."

Traditional authority, by contrast, is based on personal loyalty. Thus, loyalty to a master determines the legitimacy of a master's rule. The content of some commands may be determined by tradition, and where the content is not so stipulated, the discretion of the master is not fundamentally limited. The question for those possessing such authority is typically how far they might go before encountering concerted resistance from subjects. This sort of domination cannot be created by legislation. Staff, where this is present, may be recruited from kin (occasionally slaves or clients) or from loyal favourites. We mention traditional authority here because Weber proceeds to define it in terms of what is missing from the rational-legal/bureaucratic type. Missing are spheres of competence governed by rules, hierarchy established according to those rules, a contractual system of appointment and promotion, required technical training, and fixed salaries.

The ends of institutional action are seen as legitimate, and the means chosen are seen as appropriate. Otherwise, there could be noncompliance. If action is commanded of us, it is not only the threat of violence which makes us comply. We often believe the ends to be legitimate, although even if this is the case, our own interests (material and otherwise) cannot be undermined without our protest.

A loyal staff must be secured, and they must know what to expect from the governed. Whether we are speaking of a medieval Church, a modern business, an ancient army, or a volunteer organization, the meaning of actions and objects will be of primary importance. Which meanings of which actions and objects figure in the actions of which participants toward which ends by the selection of which means? How are the interests of all concerned served in such a way that the given state of affairs is relatively stable, so that the interests of all are, at least minimally, met?

In the case of the modern bureaucracy, participants, from top to bottom, are for the most part engaging in purposive-rational action. The most appropriate, efficient means are chosen for the achievement of a given end. In order to increase profits, produce the next widget, fix the boiler, train the troops, get a new pair of glasses, or mow the lawn, we must have knowledge of the simplest and most efficient means to achieve the task. We do not typically attempt to mow the lawn in such a way as to maximize homage to our ancestors, nor do we churn out the next widget in such a way as to appease or propitiate the local gods. Each community, institution, or value sphere will have its own set of meanings commensurate with its set of typical, legitimate ends and the appropriate means for their achievement. If all has been considered correctly, participants will believe in the legitimacy of the ends and of the rules which define the means of their attainment. Officials will be paid, customers satisfied, clients served, opponents defeated, and the grass cut.

Bureaucracy is the form of social organization in and through which rational-legal authority is exercised and maintained. It is also that form which clearly takes hold with the advent of a capitalist economic order. One does not cause the other to arise; they have a strong affinity. In fact, Weber asserts that the dominance of a money economy is important for the pecuniary compensation of unlanded officialdom and for the continued existence of such an administrative form with its preference for calculable ends.

This form is very stable since it is much less susceptible to fluctuations in agricultural yield or subjects' income for its taxation base. Although there is a strong awareness of status among officials, the impersonal character of the office integrates the whole into a disciplined mechanism. There were precursors to modern bureaucracy in ancient China, Egypt, and Rome, but bureaucracy has proven much more stable in a modern capitalist economy. "The objective discharge of business primarily means a discharge of business according to *calculable rules* and without regard for persons." (1946: 215). Emotions, which defy measurement, are systematically eliminated from business. Even cultural organizations with an apparently tenuous relation with business also demand a detached, objective expert; considerations of grace and gratitude no longer prevail.

Bureaucracy is very difficult to destroy and has become the means of carrying community action over into rationally ordered societal action. Since bureaucratic "motion" originates from the top, bureaucracies help solidify power relations. At the same time, bureaucracies make themselves indispensable to most members of society. We are dependent on their methodical functioning. Thus bureaucracy also promotes a trained obedience to rules and regulations.

Although Weber finds bureaucracy to be efficient, precise and, owing to its impersonality, rather levelling, its levelling effect falls far short of democracy; its top-down flow of not only command but interest makes it serve, in its societal and economic consequences, what he calls a crypto-plutocratic distribution of power. However, it is, in his final analysis, the most nearly perfect tool of domination yet developed.

TRADITIONAL DOMINATION
AND AUTHORITY

REMEMBER, HOWEVER, that Weber describes an ideal type. Everyone in this scenario has a near perfect knowledge of the means-end logic. Everything must have been thought of in the formulation of the rules. We can, nonetheless, recognize our lives in some of his description. We are familiar with the impersonality of bureaucracy. In some measure, this impersonality has its advantages; we do not *have* to know the registrar to be admitted to university. But, it might help. We are familiar with the adage: "It's not what you know, it's who you know." Impersonality can work toward fairness; if we are all *only* numbers, it is hard to favour one of us. On the other hand, we know that favouritism does occur.

If we were to make things much less impersonal, we would end up with what Weber calls traditional authority, and favouritism becomes, in an important sense, the name of the game. Neither the medieval Church, the Holy Roman Empire, joint-venture companies, Charlemagne's army nor a vassal securing a territory were bureaucratically organized, and did not exhibit rational-legal authority. In rare and short-lived cases, one person might tell everyone what to do in a given territory. This type of authority, which Weber called Sultanism, was very unstable. A staff, even if not bureaucratic, must be organized. Because they might be required as a means of administration, their interests must also be served. This was typically organized on the basis of personal loyalty. Often the means of administration would not be in the possession of the power-holder, and s/he would have to secure this means along with the loyalty of those who possessed it. Imagine the favours which had to be done. On many occasions, administration would be a family matter and kin were originally the most common persons solicited for this purpose. Eventually prebends, benefices, and fiefs (various forms of allowing an appointee access to incomes from a territory or community, tax farming or part of the income of a church, traditionally secured by the occupant of a particular position) would have to be offered to secure the aid of allies and staff. The economic order is central in this case, and the material interests of staff and allies had to be considered. But even these actions, in Weber's view, were insufficient in themselves to secure compliance with commands. The sanctity of tradition and the commensurate right of a person of appropriate status to issue commands is also of high importance. In terms of social action, such traditions entail the maximization of an ultimate value. Compliance with the ends and commands of a power-holder is increased, under such conditions, by reverence for sanctity and tradition. Kings, queens, and priests have been able to count on these traditional grounds for authority.

Much of Weber's discussion involves a constant movement back and forth between the pure or ideal type and actual cases from the history of China, Africa and Rome. In each case, the precise means of securing allegiance and compliance vary. But it is the ideal types which make it possible for him to locate these precise means. He may well be missing issues which are vitally important to the members of these societies, but his purpose is to explain the emergence of western forms. The transition to new forms and types has often involved the intrusion of another form of authority and form of action, charismatic authority and emotional action.

CHARISMATIC AUTHORITY

TRADITIONAL AUTHORITY has tended to block the emergence of capitalist markets in many ways. The traditional focus on the needs of rulers obstructs the non-traditional distribution of goods. Economic relations under this system are tradition-bound. Economic action tends to be oriented toward ultimate values, and productive capacity is not market oriented. The calculability of obligations and the freedom of private enterprise are lacking. How did these arise?

Changes in the character of traditional authority have occurred, and such changes have often focused on the leadership of a charismatic figure. Such a figure is thought to have exceptional, if not superhuman, qualities, by virtue of which s/he is regarded as leader. Although the recognition of such qualities is important, "the basis lies rather in the conception that it is the duty of those subject to charismatic authority to recognize its genuineness and to act accordingly. Psychologically this recognition is a matter of complete personal devotion to the possessor of the quality, arising out of enthusiasm, or of despair and hope" (1978: 242).

Charismatic authority is thus opposed to the rational rules of legal authority as well as to the time-honoured precedents of traditional authority. It tends to be revolutionary in repudiation of the past, and is often embodied in the figure of the prophet. There are no appointments, careers, or promotions. In Weber's terms, it entails a call, spiritual duty, or mission, and in its pure type is foreign to economic considerations. At the end of one of his discussions of charismatic authority, Weber (1978: 245) neatly summarizes the relations between the three types of authority:

> In traditionalist periods, charisma is *the* great revolutionary force. The likewise revolutionary force of "reason" works from *without*: by altering the situations of life and hence its problems, finally in this way changing men's attitudes toward them; or it intellectualizes the individual. Charisma, on the other hand, *may* effect a subjective or *internal* reorientation born out of suffering, conflicts, or enthusiasm. It may then result in a radical alteration of the central attitudes and directions of action with a completely new orientation of all attitudes toward the different problems of the "world." In prerationalistic periods, tradition and charisma between them have almost exhausted the whole of the orientation of action.

Weber then takes on the problem of how such a community of followers is maintained in the face of the loss of a charismatic leader. How is it, in other words, that charisma, once established, might be routinized? Both followers and administrative staff, argues Weber, have ideal and material interests in stabilizing their positions. Where actual discipleship is cut off, this creates the problem of succession.

The simplest way to solve the problem of succession is for the charismatic leader to designate a successor. A well-chosen successor can provide legitimacy with the quality of an acquired right. Personal charisma may thus be passed on and embodied by a heredity of ritual attainment of grace under the right circumstances. The majority, however, cannot continue purely on the basis of an idealistic "calling" without the daily presence of the charismatic leader. Charisma is routinized in such a way that followers or disciples regulate recruitment and secure powers and economic benefits. This situation may develop into either traditional or rational-legal authority. Norms for recruitment will be set up on one or the other basis. The corresponding positions for staff will also be set up: benefices, offices, or fiefs.

Thus, either traditionally or legally grounded status and material advantages will be instituted. In the traditional case, status differentiates those with a stake in the community from the laity. In the legal case, state officials are differentiated from tax payers. These status considerations are also economically important. Control over economic goods can be secured by certain individuals in this way.

How do followers of legitimate leaders engage in social action in such a way as to serve the maintenance of the community and of staff positions? In earlier periods, when charismatic persons were able to found or transform communities because of the instability and despair characteristic of the previous state, the maintenance of a recently founded order would demand the routinization of charisma, and this took place, typically, in either a traditional or bureaucratic way. Again, the precise details would be rather different for each individual case, but these are Weber's guidelines for a detailed analyses of such cases. Action, meaning, authority, and economic order and conditions would all have to be taken into consideration.

CLASS, STATUS, AND PARTY

Classes, status groups, and parties are phenomena having to do with the way in which power is distributed in communities. Weber defines power as "the chance of a man or of a number of men to realize their own will in a communal action even against the resistance of others who are participating in the same action" (1946: 180).

Class, according to Weber, is an economic determination; market situation is primary in determining class. Individuals may be said to occupy the same class situation when they share a similar set of opportunities in the market place. Either their assets or their training are likely to provide them with similar life chances; they will do well to approximately the same degree. Thus, classes are not actual communities (persons similarly describable in economic terms need not interact with one another nor exist in similar institutions), but this shared situation could provide a basis for communal action. Such action would depend on the perception that benefits would result from collective action. The feeling of belonging together by virtue of a shared class position may result in "societal action," a rationally motivated adjustment of interests in light of the economic order. Cultural and intellectual conditions may also help to bring about societal action. Do people rationally associate because of the given structure of the economic order?

Status, a measurement of social honour or esteem, may get in the way of communal action on a class basis. Struggles over food prices, the labour process, or debt bondage abound in history. Those who share the same status, on the other hand, are typically already a community linked by class. Status is often, however, in sharp opposition to considerations of property. Life-style, residence, fashion, marriage partners, and "circles" are often paramount considerations.

Parties are groups formed to influence communal action. They may be of any size, and their members will strive for their goals in a planned manner. Their actions may run the gamut from naked violence to canvassing. In general terms, they attempt to move persons to communal action in order to affect change in the societal and, perhaps, economic and legal order. Parties, representing different communities of interest, are typically involved in the attempt to change or maintain particular orders. The persons involved in a course of action may enjoy a communal relationship or an associative one. Relationships, furthermore, may be open or closed. Closed relationships may take place in organizations which display different types of rule, for example, political (order maintained by threat of violence by administrative staff) or hierocratic (order enforced "through psychic coercion by distributing or denying religious benefits") (Weber 1978: 54).

RELIGION, ACTION AND
MODERN RATIONALITY

IT IS only rather recently that the industrial provision of most needs has been carried out by the method of enterprise, by taking advantage of an economic, market opportunity. In such enterprises, possible income is determined by capital accounting. Books are kept and balances struck. Calculations are made on this basis in order to determine the likely profitability of a given project. The full-blown version of this method of need-provision is the result of the following:

1. the appropriation of material means of production;
2. market freedom;
3. rational technology (principally mechanization);
4. calculable law (forms of adjudication and administration which allow for predictable outcomes);
5. formally free labour (persons who voluntarily sell their labour-power but must do so to stave off starvation); and
6. the commercialization of economic life.

All these conditions are necessary ingredients in the rise of capitalism in Weber's view. We shall now turn to another ingredient, "the capitalistic spirit."

All of these descriptions, analyses, and comparisons were undertaken with a view to understanding the emergence of modern western forms of domination and rationality. Weber examines value-rational (often religious) motivational roots of impersonal orders and calculated action. Ancient societies in which there developed many of the ingredients necessary for capitalism, such as large surpluses, currency, and sophisticated mathematics, did not develop capitalism or science.

Weber conducted numerous studies of religion in various historical contexts, and it is in these studies that we find his mature account of the rise of modern, western rationality. He does this in a way which makes use of most of the concepts developed thus far. Originally, according to Weber, "religion" did not describe a type of behaviour or thought separate from other realms of life. In his view, religious and magical accounts of the world originally made causal connections between various events (fallacious connections only from the viewpoint of modern attributions of causality), and the goals of actions thus described were predominantly economic. In the earlier cases, religion served to classify activities in the practical economic realm by making sacred some particular form of practice. Where practices are sacralized, and this sacralization provides meaningful motivation for action, change is difficult. In this early instance, religion is uniquely integrated with economic practice.

Religious phenomena tend to deal with "evils and advantages in this world" (1964: 27), but they evolve, Weber argues, in such a way that the notion of god(s) is rationalized while "practical and calculating rationalism" recedes. Otherworldly goals are ultimately embodied in either priests or prophets. Priests are attached to a particular order, while prophets tend to undermine it. Prophets are further distinguishable from priests by virtue of their charismatic power and by their lack of remuneration (1964: 47)

Once a charismatic prophet arises and is successful in achieving orientation to other-worldly goals, the charisma is soon routinized into the occupational pattern typical of a priesthood. This "ethical rationalization" made it possible to predict and calculate people's behaviour since "they were attached to a cosmos of obligations" (1964: 36). A prophetic revelation offers a harmonious and integrated cosmos for ethical action within it so that "life obtain[s] a unified and significant pattern" (1964: 589). Descriptions of how the world works provide recipes for action within it. This trend toward a meaningful whole produces tensions, particularly in commercial cultures. In agrarian cultures, there is a notable lack of religious ethical rationalization (1964: 81) which makes action in all spheres conform to general ethical principles.

Weber hastens to add, however, that a particular kind of economic order is not in itself responsible for producing a particular type of ethical rationalism. Capitalism did not produce a uniform religious ethic. The relation between economic rationalism and certain types of ethically rigorous religion has appeared only occasionally outside the West. The clarification of such relations became Weber's overriding task.

In the West, the rationalization of ethics took place among the middle and lower middle classes, particularly artisans. Whereas Islam and Catholicism, in his view, reintroduced local saints and deities to satisfy and appeal to the masses (retention of traditional values), in Protestantism, the appeal to the urban lower middle class took the form of ethical congregational religion. The idea of salvation contained in such a congregational ethic appealed to the lower classes because of their disprivileged status; upper classes, on the other hand, who enjoy a privileged position, feel no need for a notion of salvation but, rather, legitimate and justify their advantageous position in the world (1964: 107).

Weber proceeds to argue that economic rationalism of the modern capitalist sort has as its attendant feature ethical congregational religion. Other societies, in spite of the presence of wealth, merchants, and multiple strata, did not develop the economically rational practices of the capitalist type. He takes a look at the religion of India, for example, to effect the kind of comparison outlined in his ideal type methodology. Having formulated the type of rational action which might be expected from a completely informed knowledge of means for the achievement of practical ends, he proceeded to attempt to identify those action elements and features of the social economic order which obstructed economic and scientific rationalism.

According to Weber, Hinduism can be characterized as the ritual attainment of purity. The rituals observed are status (caste) specific and tend to maintain the status hierarchy. Hinduism took hold and predominated, he argues, because it legitimated the power of secular power-holders. The Brahmans (priests) consecrated secular princes, and social rank was determined with reference to the Brahmans who were at the top. The growth of Hinduism in antiquity was characterized by the cooperation of secular power with religious power; this symbiosis between Brahman and prince legitimated the social order. Princes were thus also confined to working within this legitimate framework. The strict observance of dharma (caste-situated ritual) was the order of the day. State officials did not exist apart from these practices and arrangements. The rigidity resulting from caste-situated dharma prevented the formation of city-states and other forms of free association for rational, this-worldly, goal-directed activity.

Only by the most rigorous observance of dharma could individuals hope to escape the cycle of rebirth. There was no super-worldly god before whom impersonal or natural laws pertained equally to all people regardless of caste. According to Weber, these characteristics of Hinduism prevented the development of social criticism, rationalistic speculation, and the concept of natural law (1958b: 144), all of which emerged in early modern Europe.

Notice, at this point, the precise function of Weber's use of the ideal type. However, a correct analysis of meaning and action within the Brahmanic framework was not in itself satisfying to Weber. He went on to attempt to clarify what is *lacking* in this in comparison to an ideal type. The life of a Hindu can be understood, first of all, in terms of escape from the wheel of rebirth. This involves strict attention to inviolable ritual in such a way as to seem not to act. The goal is knowledge of what is eternal and unchanging in the universe. The pursuit of this goal results in a lack of attention to the physical body as it acts in social life, and as a consequence we observe within Hinduism the development of erotic and contemplative technique. Contemplation in the absence of worldly affairs takes priority.

If we can assume that this account of Hinduism is at least minimally adequate, why not leave it at that? Why go on to describe what was lacking? Weber proceeds to tell us that India, China, indeed, all of Asia, lacked a sense of empirical fact, of rational speculation and systematization, and of the "real forces of experience" (1958b: 342). Weber's attitude is typical of the Eurocentric perspectives of the nineteenth century when European powers were establishing colonies. His types were constructed, not in order to produce the definitive account of Indian society or thought, but, rather, by a comparison to Hinduism, to make possible a thoroughly systematic account of modern western action, authority, thought, and order.

A situation at least marginally analogous to that described above existed in late medieval/early modern Europe, claims Weber. Catholicism during this period did not lay much stress on the monitoring of the affairs of everyday life. It was not ethically rational in this sense. Although its ethics included notions of Christian charity and a concern for the basic needs of the earthly community, its ultimate orientation is otherworldly. Serious striving and serious thought are to be devoted primarily to the afterlife rather than to this life.

Weber terms this ethic, *other-worldly asceticism*, a form of self-denial oriented to matters not of the everyday world. To be a moral virtuoso in this culture, one removes one's self from the world in a quite literal sense. "Get thee to a monastery!" This might have been the call of the day. In fact, it is still quite common to speak of a religious vocation as a "calling." More recently, it has become commonplace to speak of worldly occupations as callings, and it is in some measure this transition which provides Weber's focus in his best known work, *The Protestant Ethic and the Spirit of Capitalism*.

Consider the discipline of the monastery, an ideal location in which to be ascetic, to deny one's self earthly pleasures. To begin with, one is literally removed (often to a mountain top) to a place far away from the source (the town) of those pleasures. The disciplined and rigorous observance of daily practices is also designed to further this other-worldly orientation. The discipline of the monastery and the disregard for everyday work in the towns provided "serious inner resistance" to the development of the kind of economic rationality and discipline required by capitalist life. The labourer's devotion to the earthly, productive tasks at hand and the entrepreneur's ceaseless efforts to streamline business and renew profit at the expense of whatever pleasures success might afford would not be aided by the other-worldly orientation of Catholicism, much less by an attempt to do all of it on a mountain top.

The demands of capitalism in terms of everyday habits, the separation of business from the household, rational industrial organization (including the attendant work-discipline), and rational bookkeeping, all represent a different orientation to everyday life and its concerns. For Weber, the acquisition of assets and a history of engagement in trade and exchange were not, in themselves, sufficient to produce the requisite daily habits of disciplined hard work and constant attention to business. Much less, could they overcome the "serious inner resistance" of Catholicism's other-worldly orientation.

According to Weber, a different ethical, religious orientation was necessary to provide the devotion to daily work which the modern capitalist economic order was just beginning to require in parts of Europe in the sixteenth century. The development of certain Protestant sects, namely Puritan ones, provided the means of overcoming the inner resistance to capitalist work habits, although they were not established with this purpose or function in mind.

The prominent charismatic figures involved in this transition were Martin Luther and John Calvin. Luther was a monk, but he had several battles with the Church. The outcome of these battles, for our present purposes, was the removal of special status for religious vocations (i.e., priests). In other words, according to Luther's doctrine, it was just as worthy, in the eyes of God, to have an ordinary, earthly occupation as to be a priest. There was no spiritual advantage, in terms of salvation, to have a religious calling rather than some other: miner, baker, merchant, carpenter. The ritual attainment of grace (the sacraments) was also much less important to Luther. (Luther also removed the Church's restrictions on usury, the loan of money at interest, arguing that one could legitimately earn as much from lending one's money at interest as one could earn by using the same funds in a different sort of business. The Church's view was that usury involved the sale of time which belonged to God and not to any human.) Thus, the status and importance of everyday, earthly work received a boost at the hand of Luther.

In Weber's account, John Calvin was of even greater importance than Luther. Whereas Luther had removed the negative connotations connected with everyday work, Calvin went much further by stipulating that it was absolutely necessary to *devote* one's self to duty in one's earthly calling. This is another form of asceticism. Weber terms it "this-worldly asceticism." Asceticism, self-denial, is still at issue; however, in this case, it does not involve one's removal from everyday life. It is, rather, as though the discipline of the monastery had been transported to the everyday life of the town.

What was at issue for Calvin was duty to God, not creating the everyday habits required by modern capitalism. The latter is, in Weber's view, simply the unintended consequence of the actions of many of Calvin's followers. For Calvin, the world was simply an utterly evil and depraved place. It was not susceptible to rational explanation, at least not of the kind of which any human being is capable. To suggest that one can understand the world and the ways of God is not only arrogant but an act of blasphemy in Calvin's eyes.

To serve and to do one's duty to God, one must simply avoid evil at all costs. How does one avoid evil? One accomplishes this through devotion to duty in one's earthly calling. "Idle hands are the devil's playthings." We cannot work our way into heaven; the ways of God are mysterious. We must simply do our duty. Ethical congregational religion, that of Calvin's later followers, in Weber's view, provided the appropriate motivation for the work habits required by capitalism, although this was far from Calvin's intention.

Calvin's doctrine of predestination was also of interest to Weber. According to Calvin, the elect, those destined to go to heaven, were chosen by God at the beginning of time. For Calvin, there was absolutely nothing that one could do about this condition, neither did one know whether one was of the elect, nor could one change the election in any way. Certain of Calvin's followers thought that one might fall from grace if one failed in devotion to work, and still others believed that success in one's earthly calling might be a sign that one was one of the elect. "Fruit does not grow on an evil tree." Here is a rational motivation to work hard. If one is successful, furthermore, this might be a sign of God's blessing.

Thus, we arrive at a kind of spiritual bookkeeping. What begins as a charismatically-led spiritual movement rooted in ascetic religious values is routinized into a rational, calculating approach to everyday, economic concerns. Labourers had a spiritual motivation for devotion to a life of toil, and entrepreneurs, from artisans to bankers, were religiously inspired to devote themselves to the growth of business rather than to enjoy its occasional fruits.

In this way, religious values provided the end (serving God) with a this-worldly ascetic practice as the means of its achievement. Religiously-motivated action did not have as its end the creation of capitalism, nor its requisite work habits, much less the acquisition of riches. "It is as easy for a rich man to pass through the gates of heaven as it is for a camel to pass through the eye of a needle." The result was, nonetheless, a devotion to work and the rational conduct of business.

The Prostestant work ethic, in Weber's view, is one of the factors which produced modern life in the capitalist West. The work ethic is still with us, along with economic and scientific rationality. Their companion factors are purposive-rational action, rational-legal authority, and bureaucratic domination. Indeed, we live in a highly rationalized "cosmos of obligations."

In his conclusion to *The Protestant Ethic*, Weber does not claim to have discovered *the* cause of capitalism and its work practices. He does want to drive home his point about the historical significance of ideal, motivating factors, ideas which proved amenable in a form adapted to the positions and needs of Calvin's followers. His ultimate conclusion is that we have become locked into what he calls "the iron cage" of rationality. If we hope to survive in the modern world, we must devote ourselves to work in a calling and in so doing become rational and calculating to a large extent.

> The Puritan wanted to work in a calling; we are forced to do so. For when asceticism was carried out of the monastic cells into everyday life, and began to dominate worldly morality, it did its part in building the tremendous cosmos of the modern economic order. This order is now bound to the technical and economic conditions of machine production which to-day determine the lives of all individuals who are born into this mechanism, not only those directly concerned with economic acquisition, with irresistible force. Perhaps it will so determine them until the last ton of fossilized fuel is burnt. (1958a: 181)

"[T]he idea of duty in one's calling prowls about in our lives like the ghost of dead religious beliefs." (1958a: 182) The religious roots have died out but we are firmly planted in the rational soil fertilized by the Puritans.

We began this chapter with an examination of Weber's work, "Politics as a Vocation," a speech delivered in 1918, and we conclude with a brief account of another speech, "Science as a Vocation," delivered in the same year. The notion of a rational, calculating ethos, originally a sort of spiritual bookkeeping oriented toward an ultimate value, is developed into a scientific as well as an economic rationality. All that is worth knowing is knowable in a systematic, measurable, calculating way. Whatever is unknowable in these terms is simply deemed unworthy of serious investigation.

> [Rationalization] means that principally there are no mysterious incalculable forces that come into play, but rather that one can, in principle, master all things by calculation. This means that the world is disenchanted.

> One need no longer have recourse to magical means in
> order to master or implore the spirits, as did the savage,
> for whom such mysterious powers existed. Technical
> means and calculations perform the service. This above
> all is what intellectualization means. (1946: 139)

Can the scientific intellect lead the way to happiness? No
one believes this any more, says Weber, "aside from a few
big children in university chairs or editorial offices" (1946:
143). Science cannot help us choose between values, nor can
it plead for a particular interest, because, in Weber's view,
"'[s]cientific' pleading is meaningless in principle because the
various value spheres of the world stand in irreconcilable
conflict with each other" (1946: 147). Science can be seen
both as within and as part of the cage; it, too, is slave to the
powerful interests which prevail in modern bureaucratic
domination, although it may have helped to determine which
interests shall have pride of place in a disenchanted world.

CONCLUSION

Modernity, Reason and the Legacy of Classical Sociological Theory

In ONE sense, the legacy of the classical sociological tradition is easily summarized: consult Marx on the economic and class bases of politics and revolution; Durkheim on the significance of symbolic features like collective representations; and Weber on modern rational organizations and their value roots. Durkheim contributed to functionalism, whereas Marx and Weber contributed in different ways to conflict theory. Of course, this summation is much too simplistic and, as far as the second claim is concerned, quite misleading. Marx treated the symbolic and intellectual in his theory of fetishism and produced a theory of how capitalist relations tended to reproduce themselves; Durkheim concerned himself with class and conflict in his look at the abnormal division of labour; and Weber was vitally interested in symbolically rooted motivations as well as structures.

If one were to select a couple of issues on which to compare and contrast the arguments of our three major thinkers, then perhaps the division of labour and religion would serve best. All three of them wrote a surprising amount on religion. Marx, although he disagreed with the foundation of the Young Hegelians' attacks on religion, sees it as an outgrowth of and a response to an essentially oppressive set of conditions and relations. Even in a mature work like *Capital*, he refers to some popular notions of the nature of the economy as religious in character. Durkheim left a rabbinical tradition and became an atheist. Weber declared himself to be "religiously unmusical." For Durkheim and Weber religion was once fundamentally important, and substantial in history but no longer is, whereas, for Marx, it never was.

All three stated that ideas could move people, but only under propitious circumstances, i.e. when the ideas satisfied
some fundamental need.

The concept of the division of labour, although Durkheim
was the only one to write a major work by that title, in fact,
appears throughout Marx's work in his discussions of the
transition from one social form of labour to another and, of
course, occupation or "calling" plays a significant role in
Weber's account of the rise of modern rational organization
of the economic order and other institutions.

According to Marx, people's practical life-activity, the way
they provide for themselves and the social relations and conditions in which this takes place, is primary. Religious notions arise as a result of specific sets of relations, and one
cannot decipher their roots without being highly specific:
particular religions arise from particular conditions. There
is no such thing as religion-in-general. Somewhat ironically,
Marx is the only one who views some modern notions as
religious in character. For Weber, even though religion (in a
way rather similar to that described by Durkheim and Mauss)
was initially very important in its function of sanctifying economic practice, it became a highly contingent affair depend-
ing, in part, on the emergence of charismatic figures. The
possibility of the emergence of a charismatic figure is now
rather unlikely, argues Weber, due to bureaucratic domination in present day life. For Durkheim, religion was virtually
identical with the external force and authority of the
collectivity. The common conscience and collective representations were vitally important in maintaining social organization and practice. As the division of labour becomes
complex, however, independent reason (science) emerges and
largely replaces religiously expressed morality and images
of the world.

Durkheim argues that in order for the division of labour
to function harmoniously as it develops into a complex system of occupations and professions, people must be justly
rewarded according to talent. For Marx, the occupational
structure of modern society is a function of the capitalist
mode of production in which there exist fundamental and

inescapable tensions. Capital accumulation tends to take precedence over everything, including "just" reward, and he observed these conditions with a view to the possibility of overcoming them. In Weber's work, the most important feature of the occupational structure is its bureaucratic character. Occupational duty had originally been a religiously inspired calling but became a matter of enforced routine in the service of powerful interests. The prospects for its harmonization or overcoming are minimal in his view.

We have considered three accounts of the rise of modern society and three differing assessments of its essential features. Briefly, for Marx, relations of exchange equivalence give rise to labour-power as a commodity. This, in turn, sets up the opposition between capital accumulation and exchange equivalence. The logic of this process appears natural and has a profound influence on thought about nature and society. For Durkheim, the rise of modern society presents a crisis of solidarity created by the rapid growth in complexity of the division of labour and the concomitant decline in community-based, religious symbols and concepts. Yet, he is much more optimistic than the others and suggests that the very same growth and decline free the intellect to extract the immanent logic of the real operation of nature and society. National educational institutions can, in his view, instruct members of society as to the real reasons for their precise role in the goal of national integration. Weber is the most pessimistic about modern society, about the possibility of the development of conditions and relations suitable for the exercise of individual freedom. Rationality, even though he chooses to understand other societies and institutions on its terms, provides the organizing principle for bureaucracy, a virtually impenetrable tool of domination for powerful interests. Religion played a role in this development but can no longer pose a threat to the bureaucratically-organized provision of essential needs.

Reason, that which the Enlightenment thinkers thought of as standard equipment of the human individual, takes different forms as, indeed, each of our three theorists suggested. How many of us think that the world is reasonable, that it is unfolding as it should? Those who favour progress have often used the concept of reason to paint a picture of the world as developing inexorably, by means of an inner logic, toward a fully understandable and controllable condition. But, as our theorists (with the possible exception of Durkheim) illustrate, the mastery and control of conditions, by whatever logic, has not come about. Contrary to both religious and scientific views, there would appear to be no overarching logic or reason according to which the world unfolds. The Enlightenment, Comte, and Spencer entertained what is now called a metanarrative, a "plot" or fabric of a story according to which everything developed and will continue to do so. In religious terms, this used to be called an "eschatology," a divine plan for the world. These, it is now suggested, are merely tools of domination, of "hegemony" in more recent terminology, and cannot guide thought in any way other than to deepen the domination.

Marx viewed religion as epiphenomenal. It could not operate as a substantial force in its own right, since it owed its emergence and salience to sets of conditions and relations which produced it and in reference to which it may function. The intelligibility of society depends on the instantiation of reasonable and intelligible conditions and relations between persons. The form of rationality by means of which we, either as members of society or as sociologists, attempt to understand society is itself confined in its effective operation to a particular set of conditions and relations. Marx's thought is devoted, in large measure, to illustrating this; he points out the ways in which capitalist conditions and relations (its logic) do not make sense. They are contradictory. Durkheim, on the other hand, argues that religion used to be the means by which people understood their world. Religion was rooted in the organization of groups and functions in society, but where intellectual specialization had not yet taken place, the authority of society (collective, moral forces) asserted itself by forming interpretations of the world which reinforced the self evidence of group practices. The growth of the division of labour, to the point where intellectual contemplation of nature is professionalized, results in the appropriation of nature's logic as human logic and proceeds, through sociology, to create institutions which reflect this logic ever more closely and whose operation can be explained to members as duty. Weber tends to view religion as a form of action and sees its unintended effect in the modern world as the ironic establishment of institutions and means of domination which preclude its continued influence. The ancients were left in mystical bondage; we are rationally bound. Charismatic authority was one of the few means of thwarting the influence of powerful interests, but in the modern condition, even this authority is doomed to be caught in the web of bureaucratic domination. For Weber, the emergence of bureaucratic domination received a boost from the rise of capitalism. It was as though they needed each other. But the formation of the requisite daily habits, to assure that members fit into this society, was rooted in irrational values.

There are, in Weber's scheme, no inexorable developments, aside perhaps from the indefinite continuation of bureaucratic domination. He viewed the results of this ironic and subtle development as fostering the opposite of the human exercise of creativity and expression which many others saw modern institutions as designed to promote. Weber even had difficulty imagining the developments and actions which could weaken the hold of bureaucratic domination. For the most part, he appears to have accepted Marx's account of capitalism's development and operation. He thought, however, that significant parts of the story had been left out. For Weber, the irrational basis of action and authority was a major factor in the development of the cage into which we are now locked.

Durkheim, however, was much more optimistic. The growth of the division of labour had enabled the satisfactory provision of needs and the means of understanding how it operated to provide everyone with a true and proper sense of his/her place in this scheme of things. Since Durkheim sees the problem of modernity as one of solidarity, he views his task as solving a crisis in professional ethics. The religious symbols which had once provided simpler societies with the means of cohesion had to be replaced by more rationally organized educational and professional institutions. Above all, science, that mode of understanding and calculation produced by modern specialization, could understand the basis of solidarity and intervene on its behalf.

The rational understanding of modern society was the major issue for all three classical thinkers. Marx and Weber, although each in his own way hoped it could be accomplished, thought it would be extraordinarily difficult to achieve. Whereas Marx considered the forms of thought and calculation developed by capitalism as insufficient for understanding capitalism itself, Weber believed that the near perfect means of calculating outcomes on behalf of powerful interests, unfortunately, created and reflected modern capitalism's mode of operation. For Durkheim, reason had arrived; for Marx, it most certainly had not; for Weber, it had taken a terrible and enduring form.

This search for a rational understanding of modern society has now been abandoned in some quarters. Notwithstanding capitalism's globalization (or more likely because of it), opposition to grand, European- or North-American centred explanations of all that takes place in the social world tend to appear as either self-serving or irrelevant. Aboriginal peoples, women, and the oppressed from every quarter object to the very attempt to establish all-encompassing theories of the practical activities of people in the most diverse of circumstances. Gender and ethnicity, in particular, are now felt to be alternative foci for appreciating the local production of interest, of relevance, in short, of knowledge. Some have come to see genuine knowledge, in fact, as knowledge which is locally produced, not knowledge which can be universally valid or applied. The concept of class has been lost in the shuffle.

Interestingly enough, none of our classical thinkers had what may be called a method. Each had a favoured set of assumptions and concepts about what was most fundamental in the operation of the social world, but none of them laid out a set of methodological protocols to be applied to any and all objects. Even Durkheim's *Rules* is devoted to justifying a set of assumptions against detractors in other spheres. Weber's *Methodology*, similarly, presents a philosophical justification of his basic approach and not a manual of procedures for the conduct of research. Marx wrote almost nothing on method. For him, there is no general method which could be applied to all objects regardless of their kind and their relations.

Nonetheless, in order to appreciate our current situation, it is important that we read these classical thinkers. Their work is an extremely good place to begin in order to assess the possibilities of adopting either a modern or a post-modern position. Their legacy is evident, most assuredly, in the formulation of the problems taken up in different ways by the new brands of thought of the late twentieth century.

Burke, Edmund. [1797] 1955. *Reflections on the Revolution in France.* Indianapolis: Bobbs-Merrill.

Comte, Auguste. 1975. *Auguste Comte and Positivism: The Essential Writings.* Edited with an introduction by Gertrud Lenzer, New York: Harper.

Durkheim, Emile. 1964. *The Division of Labour in Society.* Translated by George Simpson, New York: Free Press.

———. 1965. *The Elementary Forms of The Religious Life.* Translated by Joseph Ward Swain, New York: Free Press.

———. 1961. *Moral Education.* New York: Free Press.

———. 1938. *The Rules of Sociological Method.* Translated by Sarah A. Solovay and John H. Mueller and edited by George E. Catlin, New York: Free Press.

———. 1958. *Socialism and St. Simon.* Translated by Charlotte Sattler, Yellow Springs: Antioch Press.

———. 1974. *Sociology and Philosophy.* Translated by D. F. Pocock, New York: Free Press.

Durkheim, Emile, and Marcel Mauss. *Primitive Classification.* Translated by Rodney Livingstone, Chicago: University of Chicago Press.

Gerth, Hans, and C. Wright Mills. 1946. Introduction to *From Max Weber: Essays in Sociology.* New York: Oxford University Press.

Goldmann, Lucien. 1973. *The Philosophy of the Enlightenment.* Translated by Henry Mass, London: Routledge and Kegan Paul.

Hofstadter, Richard. 1959. *Social Darwinism in American Thought.* New York: G. Braziller.

Lovejoy, A.O. 1936. *The Great Chain of Being: A Study of the History of an Idea.* New York: Harper.

Lukes, Steven. 1975. *Emile Durkheim: His Life and Work*. London: Penguin.

Marx, Karl. 1963. *The Eighteenth Brumaire of Louis Bonaparte*. New York: International.

———. n.d. *Capital* I. Moscow: Progress.

———. 1971. *Capital* III. Moscow: Progress.

———. 1978. *The Marx-Engels Reader*. Edited by Robert C. Tucker, New York: W. W. Norton.

Nisbet, Robert. 1966. *The Sociological Tradition*. New York: Basic Books.

Spencer, Herbert. 1972. *Herbert Spencer on Social Evolution*. Edited by J. D. Y. Peel, Chicago: University of Chicago Press.

Thompson, Kenneth. 1982. *Emile Durkheim*. London and New York: Routledge.

Weber, Max. 1978. *Economy and Society* I. Edited by Guenther Roth and Claus Wittich, Berkeley: University of California Press.

———. 1946. *From Max Weber: Essays in Sociology*. Edited by Hans Gerth and C. Wright Mills, New York: Oxford University Press.

———. 1949. *The Methodology of The Social Sciences*. Edited and translated by E. A. Shils and H. A. Finch, New York: Free Press.

———. 1958a. *The Protestant Ethic and The Spirit of Capitalism*. Translated by Talcott Parsons, New York: Scribner.

———. 1958b. *The Religion of India*. Edited and translated by Hans Gerth and Don Martindale, New York: Free Press.

———. 1964. *The Sociology of Religion*. Edited by Ephraim Fischoff, New York: Free Press.

Wollstonecraft, Mary. 1974 [1797]. *A Vindication of The Rights of Woman*. New York and London: Garland.

INDEX